#1 ... UTHOR

MIKE EVANS

SATAN

YOU CAN'T
HAVE MY
COUNTRY

A SPIRITUAL WARFARE GUIDE TO SAVE AMERICA

D0967586

Satan, You Can't Have My Country

Published by TimeWorthy Books
Phoenix, AZ 85046

Design: Peter Gloege | LOOK Design Studio

Paperback:978-1-62961-086-3

This book is dedicated to YOU!

You are reading this book
because you are a God-fearing American
and love America.
With all my heart, I believe that you
and people just like you are the keys
to saving our country, America.

FOREWORD

RONALD REAGAN was running for president when I was invited to speak briefly at an event he was hosting. At the close of the evening, I commented that I thought the greatest political body in America was the Republican Party. He quickly corrected me: "Son, the greatest Party in America is not the Republican Party, but the Church. We meet once every four years, the Church meets every week." Then he added, "And, I am not worried so much about the Left Wing or the Right Wing; I want God to heal the whole bird. It is sick."

What would Mr. Reagan think of our country today? I believe he would be appalled at just how much more ill the bird has become. Its wings have been clipped; it no longer flies as high as it once did. Its feathers are molting, and it is rapidly becoming more like the extinct dodo or moa birds of earlier times. It is rapidly losing its ability to fly and is being forced to run for cover, rather than soar to the mountain peaks to avoid destruction. The once-proud eagle is in danger of becoming the proverbial ostrich, hiding its head in the sand.

After a later visit with Mr. Reagan in the White House, he invited me into the Oval Office where on a side table lay his mother's Bible. It was open to II Chronicles 7:14:

> If My people who are called by My name will humble themselves, and pray and seek My face, and turn from their wicked ways, then I will hear from heaven, and will forgive their sin and heal their land.

In the margin next to the scripture Mrs. Reagan had written, "Son, this scripture is for the healing of the nations." Ronald Reagan had placed his hand on the Bible open to that scripture when he was sworn into office the first time. As he did, the United States' humiliation ended after 444 days of hell for fifty-two hostages who had been held captive by the Iranians following the overthrow of the Shah of Iran.

At his second inauguration, Mr. Reagan placed his hand on that same scripture and during that term in office the Berlin Wall fell without a shot having been fired. It is my prayer that God-fearing men and women worldwide will seek the wisdom of that verse of scripture—knowing that God is the only One who can change a season of war into a time of peace. Satan is intent on destroying the United States of America. His desire, however, is much more inclusive: He wants to extinguish all of Mankind.

Before Ronald Reagan was elected Bible-believing Christians began to pray for America. At that time, I was privileged to serve on two executive committees: Washington for Jesus, the largest prayer event ever held in the capital; and the American Coalition for Traditional Values founded by Tim LaHaye. It mobilized American churches to unite and fight for our nation. I believe God answered our prayers; but, since those days America has slept spiritually. The purpose of this book is to issue a wake-up call. The battles being fought in America are against terrorism, and are political and economic. These must be fought and won in the spirit realm before they can be won in the natural realm.

Satan has made many feints at U.S. interests abroad, but the most devastating were the events of September 11, 2001, a day whose destruction left a scar on my heart. For the people of France, that infamous date will be Friday the thirteenth, 2015 (11/13.) Employing demon-possessed suicide bombers bent on destroying as many lives as possible, Satan took aim at the people of Paris, France, arguably one of the most liberal countries in Europe. The site of the most devastating attack was at *Bataclan,* a concert hall. Ironically, the theater had been sold by Jewish owners Pascal and Joel Laloux in September 2015. During their ownership, threats had been received from extremist groups including Army of Islam for what were labeled "pro-Israel events."[1]

The venue was hosting an American rock group, Eagles of Death Metal. The drummer wore a shirt replete with a pentagram paying homage to the object of one of their songs, "Kiss the Devil." Inside the building were approximately fifteen hundred people, swaying to the music with hands raised while listening to the words:

> *Who'll love the devil?*
> *Who'll sing his song?*
> *Who will love the devil and his song?*[2]

So many died in that building, gunned down by madmen as the words to that song rang out. It ends with the line: *I will love the devil and sing his song!* Many went there just for a fun evening with little or no thought given to the words of the tunes that would be played. Perhaps there were a few true Satan worshippers in the crowd; we may never know. Members of Eagles of Death Metal escaped the carnage visited on those who paid to hear them sing the song of Satan. They were unhurt, but it will be impossible to erase those horrific images from their minds.

Spiritual warfare plainly put in the context of this book is: God-fearing Americans going to war in prayer while understanding that battles can be fought and won in prayer in the Spirit-realm. Radical Islamic terrorists are not just refugees looking for a better life. Hell is not a figment of the imagination. Heaven is real and worthy at any cost. The time has come for God-fearing Americans to stand up and declare, "Satan, you cannot have my country!"

1

AMERICA'S FUTURE:
RUDE AWAKENING
OR GREAT AWAKENING?

The hour has already come for you to wake up
from your slumber, because our salvation
is nearer now than when we first believed.

ROMANS 13:11, NIV

I LOVE MY COUNTRY—the United States of America! As a veteran, I have proudly served this nation. I buried my best friend who died defending our freedom. For those reasons, I cannot keep silent. For more than two decades, I have seen Islamic terrorism heading, like a whirlwind, toward our shores, and finally on September 11, 2001, the first terror attack on American soil blindsided this nation.

Friends have said, "Don't be negative; people want good news. Tell them good stuff. They will not listen to doom and gloom." Well, my friends, I think they were wrong; and they could be dead wrong! America is plunging headfirst into a lake of fire, and her citizens do not even know it. The hour is too late to tiptoe through the tulips. It is beyond time to face down the Enemy whose singular agenda is to "kill, steal, and destroy!" (See John 10:10) It is time to shout this message from the housetops. If America is to be saved God-fearing Americans have to wake up, and wake up now!

The prophet Jeremiah said,

> I appointed watchmen over you and said, "Listen to the sound of the trumpet!" But they said, "We will not listen." (Jeremiah 6:17, NKJV)

The ancient prophet Ezekiel prophesied:

> Again the word of the Lord came to me, saying, "Son of man, speak to the children of your people, and say to them: 'When I bring the sword upon a land, and the people of the land take a man from their territory and make him their watchman, when he sees the sword coming upon the land, if he blows the trumpet and warns the people, then whoever hears the sound of

the trumpet and does not take warning, if the sword comes and takes him away, his blood shall be on his *own* head. He heard the sound of the trumpet, but did not take warning; his blood shall be upon himself. But he who takes warning will save his life. But if the watchman sees the sword coming and does not blow the trumpet, and the people are not warned, and the sword comes and takes *any* person from among them, he is taken away in his iniquity; but his blood I will require at the watchman's hand.' (Ezekiel 33:1-6, NKJV)

You and I are the Lord's watchmen, and we dare not hold our peace! The sad news is that preachers by the thousands in America are not crying out. I hear secular, hardened commentators, ungodly politicians and abrasive talk show hosts crying out, but too many Christians are complacent and silent.

There is no question in my mind that America is receiving its final call to repentance. If God-fearing Americans sleep, then He will judge this nation in the same way He has judged every nation that has rejected His Word, and has challenged His prophetic plan.

Jesus prophesied:

> Just as it was in the days of Noah, so also will
> it be in the days of the Son of Man. People were
> eating, drinking, marrying and being given in
> marriage up to the day Noah entered the ark.
> Then the flood came and destroyed them all.
> It was the same in the days of Lot. People were
> eating and drinking, buying and selling, planting
> and building. (Luke 17:26-28)

Residents of Sodom had no idea that the good times (like the Roaring 20's before the Great Depression) were God's final mercy call before destruction. God judged Sodom, yet Sodom had no Bible. America is the Bible capital of the world, with more houses of worship than any other country. If anyone should know what is going on, we should.

I am no prophet, but I say with Amos:

> I was neither a prophet nor a prophet's son,
> but I was a shepherd, and I also took care of
> sycamore-fig trees. But the Lord took me from
> tending the flock and said to me, "Go, prophesy
> to my people." (Amos 7:14-15)

What is the answer? Again, it is found in II Chronicles 7:14 in the word "turn." Synonymous with that are "change, convert, transform and act." It is not a passive word, but one of aggressive action. Don't stand gazing into the heavens, go! As a result of the disciples going into the world to spread the Gospel, the Apostle Paul was converted. He, then, turned the carnal Roman Empire upside-down. He did not fight with fleshly weapons of war—legalism, pride, arrogance and unbridled passions—but operated within the present-day ministry of Christ.

We're so busy struggling to live the Christian life we have little energy for outrage. "Lord, help," we cry. "Help us, Jesus!" The Bible says, "He is able (immediately) to run to the cry of (assist, relieve) those who are being tempted and tested and tried [and who therefore are being exposed to suffering]." (Hebrews 2:18 AMP) If Christ is helping, why are so many Christians going through such hellish circumstances? If Christ is helping, why are so many backsliding and being removed from church rolls? If Christ is helping, why do over 3,000 churches close each year?

"Why stand ye gazing up into heaven?" the angels asked those who had gathered to watch Jesus' ascension. (See Acts 1:11 KJV) It's time that "heaven-gazers" are converted into action figures—and I don't mean Superman, Batman, Spiderman or Aquaman! I do mean Bible-man, Prayer-man, all those who have been empowered to put on the whole armor of God and stand against the Enemy and shout, "Satan, you can't have my country!"

The White House is not the key to revival—the church house is! Jesus resides not in the White House or any other building, but within the Believer. When the Apostle Paul spoke of marriage as a union between a man and a woman, he said: "This is a great mystery: but I speak concerning Christ and the Church." (Ephesians 5:32, KJV) There is a spiritual union, an ignition point, a spark between Christ and His Church that births the manifestation of God's glory.

Let's not sit here until we die; let's go! In II Kings 7 the Israelites had been besieged by the Syrians. Four starving, leprous men who had been banished from the city decided to make a change in their lot:

> They said to one another, "Why are we sitting here until we die? If we say, 'We will enter the city,' the famine *is* in the city, and we shall die there. And if we sit here, we die also. Now therefore, come, let us surrender to the army of the Syrians. If they keep us alive, we shall live;

and if they kill us, we shall only die." And they rose at twilight to go to the camp of the Syrians; and when they had come to the outskirts of the Syrian camp, to their surprise no one *was* there. For the Lord had caused the army of the Syrians to hear the noise of chariots and the noise of horses—the noise of a great army. (II Kings 7:3b-6a, NKJV)

The outcasts—a term used by many who feel they have no voice in government—decided to no longer sit idly by while their brothers and sisters died. It was these men who alerted others inside the city that God had performed a miraculous feat; the Syrians who sought to kill them had been routed by a heavenly army! They marched into the enemy's camp, ate their fill, plundered it for gold, silver and clothing, and then decided that the Israelites holed up in fear inside the city needed to be told of God's deliverance.

My good friend, the late Rev. David Wilkerson, once preached a sermon entitled, "The Wrath of Satan Shall Praise God." In it, he proclaimed:

> The present wrath that is in the world today is beyond human nature. This wrath is a satanic

rage of the powers of darkness against the Lamb of God....When Jesus comes on the scene there is no power of hell that can stand against Him. Where sin abounds the grace of God abounds in a much greater measure. In these last days of darkness there is going to be an out pouring of divine grace on every nation. The gates of hell will not prevail against the church of Jesus Christ. The weapon for every child of God is the power of the promises [the Word] of God.[3]

King Josiah was only eighteen years old when God stirred his heart over something he read in the Scriptures. Suddenly, the young king saw that the nation had offended Almighty God, and was heading towards destruction. He cried out, "God's wrath is being stored up against us." (II Kings 22:11-13, NIV)

Josiah truly repented and led the nation back to God. For those who say, "America is immune; it will not happen here; there are too many godly people in America," I say, "Remember Israel!" God destroyed Jerusalem and the temple. There is a prophetic line over which a nation should not cross, a point at which God says, "Enough!"

Where are those who weep for America, who grieve for her sins of arrogance? Millions of professing Christians have closed their eyes to what is happening. Many preachers are even telling jokes in the pulpit, and mocking those who are weeping over impending judgment. They fail to speak against moral decadence in America and refuse to use the word "Republican or Democrat" in the pulpit for fear of being politically incorrect and causing offence. There was a time when bars in the United States were gathering places for party-goers; now it is often church groups filling that role. One morning while having my car washed I began a conversation about the Lord with a woman sitting next to me. She informed me that she had no need to hear about God, that she was a strong believer. She avowed her love for the church. The woman admitted to partying and getting drunk most every Saturday night, and then going to church on Sunday to be entertained, but without condemnation. This represents what many churches in America have become.

What happens when a nation is cursed? God's hand of protection is lifted, and the powers of Hell take free reign. God, forgive anyone who does not see the warning signs! This is the reason I have repeatedly mentioned

II Chronicles 7:14. It is an extremely hope-giving scripture, but its context is in the midst of a warning for Solomon. Look for a moment at the whole passage:

> Thus Solomon finished the house of the Lord and the king's house; and Solomon successfully accomplished all that came into his heart to make in the house of the Lord and in his own house. Then the Lord appeared to Solomon by night, and said to him: "I have heard your prayer, and have chosen this place for Myself as a house of sacrifice. When I shut up heaven and there is no rain, or command the locusts to devour the land, or send pestilence among My people, if My people who are called by My name will humble themselves, and pray and seek My face, and turn from their wicked ways, then I will hear from heaven, and will forgive their sin and heal their land. . . .But if you turn away and forsake My statutes and My commandments which I have set before you, and go and serve other gods, and worship them, then I will uproot them from My land which I have given them; and this house which I have sanctified for My

name I will cast out of My sight, and will make it a proverb and a byword among all peoples.

"And as for this house, which is exalted, everyone who passes by it will be astonished and say, 'Why has the Lord done thus to this land and this house?' Then they will answer, 'Because they forsook the Lord God of their fathers, who brought them out of the land of Egypt, and embraced other gods, and worshiped them and served them; therefore He has brought all this calamity on them.'" (II Chronicles 7: 11-14, 19-24 NKJV)

Solomon was issued a warning by Almighty God:

Now that you have built your home and your temple, don't fall into pride and think you no longer need Me. If you begin to fall away, the remedy is simple: Humbly repent, seek My face, and turn from the wickedness you are doing. I will hear your prayers and respond—forgiving your sins, and healing your land. But if you continue to defy Me, regardless of establishing your throne in wisdom on My Name, I will turn from you as you have turned from Me, and

instead of being a symbol of My goodness, you
will become a symbol of what happens to those
who forsake Me. (Paraphrase, II Chronicles 7:14)

This is valuable advice. America has more idols than Solomon could have possibly erected, including relativism and greed. With them, we have made God's laws and His compassion void and meaningless. We have turned our backs on Him by adopting abominations such as abortion and homosexuality and made them accepted practices. God said if we did that we would be given over to the reprobate minds that perform such acts. (See Romans 1:21-32) If that is the case, how far are we from acquiescing to a New World Order?

Terrorist attacks on the United States and her citizens are simply warning shots across the bow of our Ship of State. God wants His children to wake up before it is too late. He sent us the prosperity of the 1920s to show He loved us. When we failed to heed the warning, He allowed us to experience the Great Depression as a final attempt to inspire us to heed II Chronicles 7:14. But we did not. Thus it was that the world, with the United States leading the way, turned their backs on the Jews, and Hitler's genocidal extermination machine closed in on them. No one acted to help them until it was too late. A third of the world's Jewish population was lost. Look around. We are seeing the same danger arising today.

The prosperity of the 1990s did little but make us even more selfish than we were in the decades before. Then in 2001, just after we had entered the twenty-first century, we were hit with something far worse than the crash of the Stock Market on Black Tuesday of 1929. What was one of the main causes of the depression? It was buying on credit. The majority of Americans rushed to freely borrow; the economy soared because of increased consumer spending. When the debts were called in, too few had the cash to pay. America lapsed into the depression, followed by not one, but two, World Wars.

Isaiah 24:6, NIV, declares:

> Therefore a curse consumes the earth; its people must bear their guilt. Therefore earth's inhabitants are burned up, and very few are left.

The United States is staring down the barrel of a loaded gun and the sound of a ticking bomb brought by terrorists who desire only the destruction of this country. Its citizens will then be expected to pay homage to Allah or face death. What is the key to escaping judgment and making God Lord of our lives?

We read in Joshua 1:6-9, NKJV:

> Be strong and of good courage, for to this people you shall divide as an inheritance the land which I swore to their fathers to give them. Only be strong and very courageous, that you may observe to do according to all the law which Moses My servant commanded you; do not turn from it to the right hand or to the left, that you may prosper wherever you go. This Book of the Law shall not depart from your mouth, but you shall meditate in it day and night, that you may observe to do according to all that is written in it. For then you will make your way prosperous, and then you will have good success. Have I not commanded you? Be strong and of good courage; do not be afraid, nor be dismayed, for the Lord your God *is* with you wherever you go."

Three times in this portion of scripture God reiterates, "Be strong and of good courage." How were His people to do that? Was it with calisthenics at sunrise or with courage pills for breakfast? Not at all! The key to God's admonition is found in verse 8: The Book of the Law, the Word of God. The people were to meditate on it, ruminate on it, deliberate on it, and contemplate it, until it became an integral part of their lives. They were to study the Words of God, memorize them, and as Deuteronomy 6:8, ESV, reminds us:

> You shall teach them diligently to your children, and shall talk of them when you sit in your house, and when you walk by the way, and when you lie down, and when you rise.

God has not changed; He said in Malachi 3:6, "I am the Lord, I do not change." If we in the United States wish to continue to enjoy success and prosperity and to experience the protection of God Almighty, the gold standard is to return to the law of God—and to meet Him in His grace and mercy.

There are times in the Bible where God used a committed individual to make a decided transformation. Daniel, Joseph, David, Elijah—all were destined to make a difference through intercession and obedience. We need only to look back at Joshua and the Israelites as they entered the Promised Land. When they were faced with Jericho, God asked only for obedience to His precise instructions: March and be quiet, then blow the trumpet and shout! How that must have vexed some who thought they had a better idea. As a result of doing exactly what God had instructed, the walls fell and the people prevailed. Apart from God, the victory could never have been won. Can we apply that to America, as did those patriots who desired freedom from King George III? The British were better trained, had more troops and certainly were better armed. As the British regulars faced off against the colonial militia, it must have looked for all the world like David slinging stones at Goliath—yet the revolutionary war was won by ill-equipped men with a mission.

In 1775 at the Virginia Convention, Patrick Henry, attorney, planter and politician delivered this resounding speech as a clarion call to stand up to the tyranny of the king:

> There is a just God who presides over the destinies of nations, and who will raise up friends to fight our battles for us. The battle, sir, is not to

the strong alone; it is to the vigilant, the active, the brave. . . .Is life so dear, or peace so sweet, as to be purchased at the price of chains and slavery? Forbid it, Almighty God! I know not what course others may take; but as for me, give me liberty or give me death![4]

After the dust had settled and the dead were buried; after the war had been won, George Washington stood humbly before those assembled, placed his hand upon the Holy Bible and took the oath of office to become the first president of the United States of America. As his voice died away, he leaned down and kissed the Bible, and then led the group in a two-hour gathering for worship. In his Inaugural address in 1789, President Washington proclaimed:

In tendering this homage to the Great Author of every public and private good, I assure myself that it expresses your sentiments not less than my own; nor those of my fellow-citizens at large, less than either. No people can be bound to acknowledge and adore the Invisible Hand which conducts the affairs of men more than the people of the United States.[5]

The men who were instrumental in founding this land of ours were unafraid to state unequivocally that the nation had been founded on biblical principles under the hand of the God of the Bible.

After Joshua led the Children of Israel into the land that God had promised to the descendants of Abraham, Isaac and Jacob, the people experienced the hand of God at work on their behalf. And yet, by the end of the book of Judges, the scribe records one of the saddest verses in the Bible in chapter 21, verse 25, "In those days Israel had no king; everyone did as they saw fit."

Can you see the correlation between the Children of Israel then and the United States today, a nation awash in situational ethics and moral relativism; a nation with no absolutes—an "anything goes" society? Where are the sacred foundations upon which this country was built? Rather than embrace them, politicos are intent on rewriting history to delete as much of our godly heritage as possible.

Evangelist Dr. Phil Hoskins stated, "America is at a crossroads and I feel that as a nation we face two possibilities, retribution or revival."[6]

PRAYER FOR AMERICA:

JOEL 3:12 ....Let the nations be awakened!

ISAIAH 1:2 ....Let the earth hear the voice of the Lord!

PSALM 9:20 ....Judge the nations in Your sight, Father, and put them to fear,

PSALM 9:20 ....that they might know themselves to be but men.

ROMANS 8:22 ....Father, the whole creation groans and labors

ROMANS 8:21 ....to be delivered from the bondage of corruption,

ROMANS 8:21 ....into the glorious liberty of the children of God.

JOHN 15:26 ....Send forth Your Spirit of Truth to bear witness of You,

JOHN 16:8 ....and to convict the world of sin, of righteousness, and of judgment.

EZEKIEL 14:6 ....Cause them to repent and to turn from their idols.

HAGGAI 2:7 ....Shake the nations, so they will come to the Desire of All Nations (Jesus).

NUMBERS 23:24 ......Father, cause Your people to rise up.

JOEL 3:11 ....Gather Your mighty ones to prepare for war.

JOEL 3:14 ....Bring the multitudes into the valley of decision.

JEREMIAH 49:14 ......Send Your ambassadors into all the nations.

COLOSSIANS 4:3 ......Open to them a door for the Word, to speak the mystery of Christ,

MATTHEW 24:14 ......that the gospel of the kingdom may be preached in all the world.

PSALM 111:6 ....You have declared to Your people the power of Your works,

PSALM 111:6 ....in giving them the heritage of the nations.

PHILIPPIANS 2:10 ....Let every knee bow and every tongue confess that Jesus is Lord!

ISAIAH 61:11 ....Cause righteousness and praise to spring forth.

HABUKKAH 2:14 ......Let the earth be filled with the knowledge of the glory

HABUKKAH 2:14 ......of the Lord as the waters cover the sea.

ISAIAH 43:9 ....Father, gather the nations together,

PSALM 22:27...........that they may worship Thee,

PSALM 46:10...........and exult Thee in all the earth.

GALATIANS 3:8........Let all the nations be blessed through Your people,

ZECHARIAH 14:14.....and let the wealth of the heathen be gathered together

2 KINGS 22:5 ....and be delivered into the hands of Your people for the work of the Lord.

ISAIAH 49:6 ....Send forth Your salvation to the ends of the earth,

MARK 12:36 ....and make Your enemies to be Your footstool.[7]

2

URGENTLY NEEDED:
ANOTHER GREAT AWAKENING

*Awake, you who sleep, Arise from the
dead, And Christ will give you light.*

EPHESIANS 5:14, NKJV

FROM THE TIME the disciples were dispersed after
the Ascension recorded in Acts 1, God has been trying
to get the attention of the Church. There have been two
events labeled "the Great Awakening," one led by such
evangelists as Jonathan Edwards, George Whitefield, and
Gilbert Tennent; the second was introduced by such men
as Charles Finney, Barton Stone, Henry Ward Beecher,
William Seymour and Peter Cartwright.

A revival swept across America beginning in the 1800s;
it was the beginning of the Second Great Awakening.
Revivalists Peter Cartwright, Charles Finney and others

led the charge, and they, along with mainline denominations such as the Methodists, joined in the revolt against the more sedate and sober versions of Christianity. It was they who birthed the circuit rider, in an attempt to reach those intrepid settlers who had moved westward across the vast land that was America.

The Second Great Awakening was a return of revival popular in the early eighteenth century. The renewed pursuit of personal holiness was characterized by the notion of the God-called common man, who carried the Gospel to his friends and neighbors. This was in sharp contrast to the highly educated theologians who led their congregations in established churches. The revival took on various forms: community involvement in the northeast region; the establishment of new denominations west of New York City; and the introduction of camp meetings in the Appalachian territory of Kentucky and Tennessee. Camp meetings were usually held yearly, and widely scattered settlers gathered for several days to enjoy the singing, preaching, and fellowship that was often denied them due to distance. It was a respite from solitary life on the frontier. The evangelical fervor experienced in the more westerly regions far surpassed the more reserved meetings in the East. Probably the largest camp meeting of that time was the one that took place in August of 1801, at Cane Ridge, Kentucky. It was estimated that up to 25,000 people made the trek to gather there.

In his own journal, Peter Cartwright wrote:

> Somewhere between 1800 and 1801, in the upper part of Kentucky, at a memorable place called "Cane Ridge," there was appointed a sacramental meeting by some of the Presbyterian ministers, at which meeting, seemingly unexpected by ministers or people, the mighty power of God was displayed in a very extraordinary manner; many were moved to tears, and bitter and loud crying for mercy. The meeting was protracted for weeks. Ministers of almost all denominations flocked in from far and near. The meeting was kept up by night and day.
>
> Thousands heard of the mighty work, and came on foot, on horseback, in carriages and wagons. It was supposed that there were in attendance at times during the meeting from twelve to twenty-five thousand people. Hundreds fell prostrate under the mighty power of God, as men slain in battle. Stands were erected in

the woods from which preachers of different Churches proclaimed repentance toward God and faith in our Lord Jesus Christ, and it was supposed, by eye and ear witnesses, that between one and two thousand souls. . . happily and powerfully came to God during the meeting. It was not unusual for one, two, three, and four to seven preachers to be addressing the listening thousands at the same time from the different stands erected for the purpose.[8]

As circuit-riding preachers and evangelists moved west, missionary organizations sprang up to fill the void left by a lack of established denominations. The American Missionary Society, American Bible Society, and the American Tract Society were just three such groups formed to aid the spread of the Gospel. Community involvement in the eastern states had produced groups whose members supported abolition (of slavery), temperance (no alcohol), and suffrage (the right of women to vote).

Charles G. Finney, known as an innovative and oft-imitated evangelist, was a strong advocate for abolition. He convincingly preached that the Gospel of Jesus Christ would save people, but that the result of salvation would be involvement in reforming one's surroundings. He urged people to become engaged in order to effect change.

The Second Great Awakening had a profound impact on the young country, even after its passion and enthusiasm had faded. Its influence was felt in the formation of new denominations, a more democratic society, and in the building of orphanages, schools, universities, hospitals, and programs to assist the poor. As one after another began to share the Good News with their neighbors, people began to witness God's grace and mercy.

There is a long line of preaching greats about whom author Max Lucado wrote in his book *And the Angels Were Silent*:

> . . . a nineteenth-century Sunday school teacher. . . led a Boston shoe clerk to Christ. The teacher's name you've never heard: Kimball. The name of the shoe clerk: Dwight L. Moody. Moody became an evangelist and had a major influence on a young preacher named Frederick B. Meyer. Meyer began to preach on college campuses and while doing so, he won J. Wilbur Chapman [as a follower of Christ]. Chapman became involved in the YMCA and arranged for

a former baseball player named Billy Sunday to come to Charlotte, North Carolina, for a revival. A group of Charlotte community leaders were so enthusiastic afterward that they planned another campaign and brought Mordecai Hamm to town to preach. In that revival a young man named Billy Graham yielded his life to Christ. . . . No sower of small seeds can know the extent of his harvest.[9]

The Old Testament admonition to King Solomon by the Lord after the dedication of the Temple energized these fiery new evangelists. Again, we return to II Chronicles 7:14, NKJV:

> If My people who are called by My name will humble themselves, and pray and seek My face, and turn from their wicked ways, then I will hear from heaven, and will forgive their sin and heal their land.

From the time Solomon first heard those words, they became an invitation to God's people everywhere. Americans wanted their land to be healed and God's will to be done; Europeans prayed for healing and for

God's favor. Christian preachers and exhorters from the two continents worked to bring the people back into a relationship with the Creator. Christians drawn to the Second Great Awakening also believed that it would usher in the return of the Messiah. But still, many in America hardened their hearts.

Today, a battle is being fought between darkness and light, between heaven and hell, between God and Satan. This is a sure sign that Jesus is coming soon! The Bible mentions: ". . . the sons of Issachar, men who understood the times." (See Genesis 12:32) God is calling prophetically to His remnant that understands the times. It is a call to prayer and repentance.

For more than three decades I have seen this battle coming and have been crying out. But many seeker-friendly pastors mocked me (as they did in the times of Noah). I cried out that the prayer shield of God's protection was being lifted from our nation; that New York City and its tallest building would be targeted.

The battle has not been won. Judgment like a tidal wave is rolling toward America. Only the remnant that hears what the Spirit is saying can stop this coming inferno. We are living in dangerous days, when men's hearts are failing them for fear. The Bible tells us to be like the wise Virgins, not the foolish ones, and to prepare for His coming. The Bible says we can know the season and times, even if we know neither the day nor the hour. We are in the last days. Look up, for our redemption draws near!

The United States of America needs another Great Awakening. I cannot afford to be silent and neither should you. The Scriptures call upon us to speak out. In Isaiah 62:1, NKJV, we read:

> For Zion's sake I will not hold My peace, And for Jerusalem's sake I will not rest, Until her righteousness goes forth as brightness, And her salvation as a lamp *that* burns.

America's very existence is a gift from God Almighty, yet this alone cannot deter an attack by Satan. The greatest superpower in world history will wake up one day in total shock, because of pride and arrogance, as did the generation on Black Tuesday when the Great Depression hit, and on September 11. The Church urgently needs to wake up, to intercede for our beloved country, so that we are ready for that day rather than to be caught sleeping.

Many churches in the United States have forsaken

intercessory prayer and the Word, and have lost the fear of God. New Age-driven congregations are rapidly morphing into the first Church of Sodom—where anything goes. Additionally, a deadly philosophy that has gripped the church for decades has been resurrected. Its teaching is that the literal Israel of the Old Testament has been replaced by the New Testament Church. This lie has been devised to relieve Christians of any responsibility towards the Jews as God's Chosen People. It is called "Replacement Theology" and was exactly what silenced the church in Germany during World War II as the death camps sped into full swing. The parishioners felt they had no obligation to the Jews who were "suffering for their sins of rejection the Messiah." It was as if Jesus' death cut them free from these people rather than grafted them into their tree. However they saw it, it was this insidious virus—an invisible moderate anti-Semitism—that allowed the mainstream Church to look the other way as the most horrific and ungodly things were unleashed.

This devious teaching did not end when Germany surrendered to end the war; it is alive and well in today's Church in America. Today the message of the coming of the Lord is seldom preached from pulpits. Many pastors fail to preach on the Ten Commandments for fear of offending someone, and would never preach about moral purity and act as if hell doesn't exist. Polluted prophets of America are also deceiving the sheep, leading them to the slaughter with their demonic Replacement Theology.

The Bible warns again and again in Revelation 22: "Behold, I am coming quickly!" Pastors have forsaken the preaching of the coming of our Lord and Savior from their pulpits. Calls to salvation have been replaced with feel-good sermons designed to do exactly what Timothy warned: "For there is going to come a time when people won't listen to the truth but will go around looking for teachers who will tell them just what they want to hear. [The King James says the people have 'itching ears.']" (II Timothy 4:3, LB)

The New Age doctrine from hell proclaiming that the Church is spiritual Israel not only takes away from the Word of God, but also feeds Jew-hatred and is robbing the Church of its eternal purpose: the great commission of being a witness in Jerusalem, Judea, and Samaria; and of hearing God—instead of blindly cooperating with the powers of darkness intent on destroying America and Israel. Those that buy into these lies are writing their own

Bible, one that rejects the words of a holy and righteous God. The New Age Church rejects God's eternal promises to Israel and arrogantly proclaims that it is God's chosen people.

The blind entertainers who espouse this theology fill their Sundays with unscriptural doctrines of man with messages drawn from secular songs, quotes from movie stars, or late-night television hosts. Yet, in their hands, they hold the Holy Bible, written by Jews who were aware of every prophetic truth concerning Israel ever inscribed. Many Americans beheld with horror the murderous events of September 11, and wept. They attended church with renewed fervor, but merely weeks later went back to sleep spiritually.

Immediately following the 9-11 attacks, politically correct spin doctors were hard at work to avoid calling a terrorist a terrorist. Some objected to the use of the words *Islamic* or *Muslim* in describing these mass murderers. Others avoided even speaking the word *terrorist*. While the American public was traumatized and paralyzed by those horrific events, members of the American press were locked in debate over how not to offend a particular segment of society.

I was invited to a live debate on the ABC affiliate in Dallas. Before anyone had determined who the terrorists were in the airliners, I stated that it was al Qaeda and that there were approximately twenty involved. I was pulled off the air and told that I could not say that; that no one knew who the perpetrators were. Terror has spread like the Ebola virus all while a blind world still refuses to even say who the enemy is: radical Islam.

Before the dust had settled over New York City and the fires were extinguished at the Pentagon, these PR experts were outlining a campaign to thwart any attempt to find those responsible for the carnage. The U.S. was declared guilty of aggression, having somehow deserved the attacks due to perceived ills against Islam and/or its adherents. Why is it so hard to place the blame precisely where it belongs, on a group of radical Islamists spouting their hate-filled ideology and killing innocent people?

Nineteen men merely sauntered aboard four airliners loaded with passengers—men, women, and children—and took control of those giants of the air. They then murdered not only the passengers but thousands of other innocent bystanders without ever looking them or their families in the eye. That is a cowardly act!

Yet another writer took Americans to task for the upsurge in patriotism and the number of American flags that were raised in the days immediately following the terrorist attack. The flag was purported to be a visual symbol of bigotry, criminality, hatred, and even homophobia in America.

Novelist Barbara Kingsolver jumped into the mêlée with this liberal, enlightening pronouncement:

> Patriotism threatens free speech with death. It is infuriated by thoughtful hesitation, constructive criticism of our leaders and pleas for peace. It despises people of foreign birth who've spent years learning our culture and contributing their talents to our economy. It has specifically blamed homosexuals, feminists and the American Civil Liberties Union. In other words, the American flag stands for intimidation, censorship, violence, bigotry, sexism, homophobia, and shoving the Constitution through a paper shredder? Who are we calling terrorists here?[10]

Statements such as these only provide ammunition for the New Age doctrine from hell that many espouse. The curses of Deuteronomy 28 are speeding inexorably toward the United States while the blessings found in the same chapter are being snatched away. How can we halt the curses while reaping the blessings?

These scriptures are a wake-up call from Heaven:

Blessed is the one who stays awake and keeps his garments, lest he walk about naked and men see his shame and they gathered in a place which is called Har Magedon. (Revelation 16:12-16)

And there will be distress such as never occurred since there was a nation until that time; and at that time your people, everyone who is found written in the book, will be rescued. (Daniel 12:1)

This is the midnight hour. If God's remnant sleeps, America will perish! However, if we choose instead to wake up and become once again the Church God called us to be, the hope we have before us is far greater than anything we have seen in the past.

I'm telling you the truth—Jesus is coming back, and He is coming back soon! Just how ready we are for that day will make all the difference in eternity.

When Believers take up the battle cry against the

host of fallen angels that were cast to earth along with Satan, the fight will be against "spiritual wickedness in high places." (Ephesians 6:12, KJV) It is these demonic creatures flooding the world with lack of knowledge, sin, and desolation, and it is these forces that can only be defeated with the Word and with intercessory prayer.

PRAYER FOR AMERICA:

Lord,

I come before Your throne and I bind every principality and power that is trying to destroy my beloved country, the United States of America. I love this country. This nation was born through intercession, prayer, sacrifice and biblical principles. We cry out as the Psalmist did: "Will You not revive us again, That Your people may rejoice in You?" Father, I pray that every demonic spirit will be bound in the mighty name of the Lord, and that You would pour out a river of healing upon our land. Heal our land, Precious Father.

SCRIPTURES FOR STUDY:

Joel 2:8

Isaiah 57:15

Psalm 138:7

Romans 13:11

Psalm 1:1-6

Psalm 85:6

Habakkuk 3:2

Joel 2:25

Ephesians 5:14

Acts 10:34-35

3

IS AMERICA A CHRISTIAN NATION?

*The Lord brings the counsel of the nations to
nothing; He makes the plans of the peoples of no
effect. The counsel of the Lord stands forever,
The plans of His heart to all generations. Blessed
is the nation whose God is the Lord, The people
He has chosen as His own inheritance.*

PSALM 33:10-12, NKJV

THE PILGRIMS, our forefathers who first colonized
what would one day become the United States of America,
purposed in their hearts to be a force for good on the earth
as defined by the Bible and its prophecies. As stated in the
Declaration of Independence, those early leaders believed
these truths to be "self-evident, that all Men are created
equal, that they are endowed by their Creator with certain
unalienable Rights that among these are Life, Liberty and

the Pursuit of Happiness." Thomas Jefferson, one of the writers of that Declaration, further posited:

> Can the liberties of a nation be secure when we have removed a conviction that these liberties are the gift of God? That they are not to be violated but with his wrath?[11]

From this first declaration, and by invoking the blessings of God in its foundations, the framers of the United States of America's constitution placed its existence and its future into the hands of God.

At that point America stepped into an alliance with God's Chosen People. This decision would eventually lead this country to be a key player in bringing about the most significant prophetic event in nearly two millennia—the rebirth of the nation of Israel.

Though scholars debate whether or not the United States was founded as a Christian nation, it is difficult to look at the writings of our founding fathers and not hear their faith echo down through the corridors of time. It is sufficient to say that until the latter half of the twentieth century this argument would never have been raised. In fact, in 1892, in the case of *Church of the Holy Trinity vs.*

United States the Supreme Court ruled that the Church has precedence over federal law, because "This is a Christian nation." In the opinion written by Mr. Justice Brewer, the court felt that:

> . . . no purpose of action against religion can be imputed to any legislation, state or national, because this is a religious people. This is historically true. From the discovery of this continent to the present hour, there is a single voice making this affirmation. . . . [12]

From there the Justice went on to cite various examples of America's connection to Christianity. He recounted documents ranging from the foundational principles set forth for the colonies to the constitutions of several states to a myriad of court cases supporting biblical principles. These all supported Christianity as the basis for law and government. One argument from the State of Pennsylvania even went so far as saying that the defense of Christianity was a necessity; the defense of the religions of the imposters such as Muhammad and the Dali Lama was not. From these precedents, Mr. Justice Brewer had this to say in his concluding remarks:

These and many other matters which might be
noticed, add a volume of unofficial declarations
to the mass of organic utterances that this is a
Christian nation.[13]

My, how times have changed! If the Supreme Court
of our nation found this to be "a Christian nation" even
116 years after the Declaration of Independence, then it is
odd that we might believe otherwise today. Somewhere
along the way we lost contact with our biblical roots—our
moral compass was replaced by moral relativism and the
ship of our great nation began its drift off-course.

Therefore, it is not surprising to see that the Christian
men who set the foundations of our nation felt an ingrained
bond with the displaced and disbursed nation of Israel
in their day. For one instance, near the beginning of the
American Revolution, when colonial soldiers were poorly
armed, starving to death, and on the verge of defeat, Hyman
Solomon, a Jewish banker from Philadelphia, went to his
brethren in America and Europe, and gathered a gift of one
million dollars for the support of the American troops. He
presented this money to General George Washington who
used it to buy clothing and arms to outfit the American

soldiers. To show his appreciation, Washington had the engravers of the U. S. one dollar bill include a memorial to the Jewish people over the head of the American eagle. Look closely at the bill; you will see thirteen stars over the eagle's head that form the six-pointed Star of David, and around that is a cloudburst representing the glory in the tabernacle of Moses. President Washington specified that this was to be a lasting memorial to the Jewish people for their help in winning the war.

While America was a Christian nation at its inception and a Christian nation through the Civil War, can the same be said today? If we are not "living for our God," what does that bode for any upcoming conflict? Has the hand of God that protected George Washington and the United States through World Wars I and II been removed? After the attack on September 11, 2001 we would definitely have to answer in the affirmative.

The United States was built on Christian principles with the Ten Commandments and the Bible as the basis for its own laws. The newly-born nation rejected tyranny, creating a constitution of checks and balances to control government power, and also refused to embrace old world struggles—such as that of Christian against Jew. The fledgling government took literally the Scripture, "Old things are passed away; behold, all things are become new." (II Corinthians 5:17, NIV)

This admonition was the true source of the idea of "separation between church and state," that all faiths would have the right to the freedom of religious gathering, worship, and expression. The State would neither dictate what church you attended nor would it silence anyone from expressing their faith in public office or the halls of government.

The founding fathers saw no conflict between these freedoms and openly expressing their religious beliefs as they went about daily business as citizens and civic leaders. They would not silence any religion for the sake of those who chose not to believe in God at all. The government was not to be anti-religious, amoral or secular as our courts seem to espouse today. It was rather to be based on Judeo-Christian virtues of love and a dedication to pray for others rather than trying to force them to change.

A feeling of kinship of spirit with the Jews by early American founders was taken to a deeper, more active, and prophetic loyalty in 1814. At a dire point during the War of 1812, Americans caught a glimpse of what this country would grow to become just over a century later: a nation integral to the rebirth of Israel. This happened when a Presbyterian pastor in Albany, New York named John McDonald made a startling discovery while teaching on Old Testament prophecy to his congregation. He had been focusing on the prophecies in the book of Isaiah, which spoke of the restoration of the nation of Israel and the subsequent redemption of humankind. One day while poring over Isaiah 18, he read a challenge to "the land shadowing with wings, which is beyond the rivers of Ethiopia: That sendeth ambassadors by the sea." (Isaiah 18:1-2, NIV)

In this he felt that "beyond Ethiopia" meant a nation far to the west of Israel, which was where Isaiah spoke these words. It was a nation shadowed by wings—a nation whose symbol was a great bird—like the bald eagle, perhaps—that sent its ambassadors by sea—what other nations were forced to send their ambassadors across the sea besides those on the continent of North America? In MacDonald's eyes this prophetic nation took shape—it had to be the United States! And what was the challenge to this nation? "Go, ye swift messengers, to a nation scattered and peeled, to a people terrible from their beginning hitherto; a nation meted out and trodden down, whose land the rivers have spoiled! . . . In that time shall the present be brought unto the Lord of hosts . . . to the place of the name of the Lord of hosts, the mount Zion." (Isaiah 18:2, 7, NIV)

In Isaiah 18, MacDonald heard a clear clarion call from God for the great nation of the United States to send ambassadors to help reestablish a kingdom for the Jewish people upon Mt. Zion in Jerusalem.

While Washington and other founding fathers had called the Jews friends and allies of our nation and oversaw the founding of America as a parallel to the Jews coming to possess their promised land of Canaan, MacDonald had seen in the scriptures a divine call to champion the Jews in regaining their own nation; not just anywhere in the world as was initially projected by early Zionists, but in the original Holy Lands with Jerusalem as its capital. In his eyes, America was the nation of prophecy that would aid the Jews in reestablishing the nation of Israel!

It is quite possible that the Damascus incident of 1840 had opened Americans' eyes—those of both Jew and Christian—to the need for the Hebrew people of the world to have a homeland within whose borders they could finally find security from persecution. The incident was the epitome of the Old World prejudices the United States had been trying to escape. It was the first time our government, especially the State Department, acted on behalf of the Jews without first being prodded by the American people. That remains true even today.

What had brought the event to the attention of President Martin Van Buren and his Secretary of State, John Forsyth, was a dispatch from the American consul in Beirut describing the massacre in Damascus of Jewish men, women, and children who had been accused of "blood libel"—a falsely claimed ritual murder in order to obtain Christian blood for Passover services. The accusations were employed as a justification to destroy Jewish property and murder Jews in the streets. In the end, it was found that French agents had started the rumor to incite Muslims in that region against the Jews and to enhance France's position as the protector of Christians in the area. While the issue was undeniably a gross violation of basic human rights, the end result was that it placed the United States unequivocally and officially on the side of the Jews, forcing the U.S. to express through formal diplomatic channels its support. This action happened so quickly that by the time the American public raised the issue to the government, formal protests had already been lodged.

Then-British Foreign Secretary, Lord Henry John Temple Palmerston, also supported the Jews. He was one of the first government officials to step out to aid Jews in Palestine by extending consular protection to them. Another Englishman, Sir Moses Montefiore took a series of journeys about this time and became a new "Nehemiah" in his charitable work aimed at aiding Jews living in Palestine.

The 1830s and 1840s also saw a great influx of Jews into the United States from Central Europe. The unrest that incited these families to seek new hope in America was also a herald of what would happen over the next century. "The Jewish Problem"—i.e., the displaced nation of Israel scattered among the nations without a land to call their own—would be an issue of debate that would fuel the Zionist movement. It would eventually lead to Hitler's attempted "final solution to the Jewish problem" in the death camps of Eastern Europe.

Thus, roughly a century before Israel's rebirth, the groundwork had already been laid in the American conscience for support of and relationship with the offspring of Isaac. The call had begun for America to be an international ambassador to help the Jews reestablish the land

and a state for themselves. Over the next century almost every American President would be faced with the issue of being part of or ignoring those prophecies.

The conundrum has continued through the decades following Israel's rebirth in 1949: Do U.S. presidents support the Jewish state or those who have vowed to destroy it? Satan has skillfully utilized this wedge to turn men sworn to uphold freedom and democracy against the very nation that holds the key to Bible prophecy. The Enemy's tactics have been subtle in some instances; devastating in others. Believers have too often stood by wringing their hands in disbelief rather than bowing before Almighty God in intercession. Rather than crying in outrage, "Satan, you can't have my country!" we cower in fear, failing to recognize the truth found in II Chronicles 7:14, NKJV:

> If My people who are called by My name will humble themselves, and pray and seek My face, and turn from their wicked ways, then I will hear from heaven, and will forgive their sin and heal their land.

We can't convince a lost and dying world to embrace

the truth of God's Word until we deal with the bad news—that we, God's people who have been called by His name, have not humbled ourselves. We have failed to pray. We have not sought His face. We have not repented from our wicked ways.

Yet, God's people are still determined to be of no personal reputation so that Christ might be all in all, Lord of Lords, and King of Kings. God is cultivating a people who are hungry and thirsty to give up the low life of being people-pleasers to attain the life of Christ. Dare I suggest that Believers seek out this trait in those men and women who are voted into office?

A lost and dying world will cry out for what we have when they see that we have been with Jesus. It will not be because of what we say, but by the glory of God manifested through our private and public lives. The heavens will open when the flesh surrenders to the present-day ministry of Jesus Christ, allowing God to rule and reign. If anything can make us despise our sinful flesh, it is the true revelation of the price Christ paid at the cross. If the Christian life can be lived in the flesh, then Jesus died in vain.

Being with Jesus applies to those who ardently pursue His Presence; His private Presence has always come before expressions of His public power. Noted author E. M. Bounds said of kneeling before the Almighty:

> God shapes the world by prayer. The more pray-
> ing there is in the world the better the world
> will be, the mightier the forces against evil.[14]

Every time the world has seen a glimpse of Jesus from one of the great revivalists, people have repented. Imagine what would happen if the world could see the life of Jesus in millions of Christians whose fires daily burn brightly! Satan fears that the Body of Christ will learn to love the smell of burning flesh consumed by the fire of the Holy Spirit, because it will release the glory of God that the world has too seldom seen. It is that glory which must come before Jesus returns. God is waiting on us to wait upon Him.

PRAYER FOR AMERICA:

Father,

Your word says, "I exhort therefore, that, first of all, supplications, prayers, intercessions, and giving of thanks, be made for all men; For kings, and for all that are in authority." I pray that our leaders would repent and that their hearts would be turned toward You; that they would seek Your face for the proper way to lead America, and that the result would be godly lives and a renewed love for You. Help Your people to choose men and women who walk after Your precepts to govern this land.

SCRIPTURES FOR STUDY:

I Timothy 2:1-3   Proverbs 2:10-12

Psalm 1   Acts 26:18

II Chronicles 10:4   Romans 13:1

Daniel 2:20-23   Psalm 22:28

Matthew 12:25   Proverbs 28:2

4

IN THE EYE OF THE PROPHETIC STORM: FROM EAGLE TO OSTRICH

It is in vain, sir, to extenuate the matter.
Gentlemen may cry, "Peace, Peace"—but there
is no peace.[15] The war is actually begun!
. . . Our brethren are already in the field!
Why stand we here idle?[16] What is it that
gentlemen wish? . . . Is life so dear, or peace
so sweet, as to be purchased at the price of
chains and slavery? Forbid it, Almighty God!
I know not what course others may take; but
as for me, give me liberty or give me death!

PATRICK HENRY
MARCH 23, 1775 / SECOND VIRGINIA CONVENTION
ST. JOHN'S CHURCH IN RICHMOND

Christ has liberated us to be free.
Stand firm then and don't submit again
to a yoke of slavery.

GALATIANS 5:1, HCSB

PATRICK HENRY STOOD before the group gathered at St. John's Church in Richmond, Virginia and delivered those stirring words. He knew the response of the colonists would be fight or flight. They could make preparations, stand firm and face down the enemy, or they could cower in fear, turn and run. Today, in this country whose freedoms were so hard-won, the challenge is the same: Will you stand firm and face down Satan, the Enemy of your soul, or will you throw up your hands and surrender to his wiles and plans for your destruction?

Those striving to achieve political correctness are working diligently to dumb-down God-fearing Americans. It began immediately following the catastrophic events of September 11, 2001 with the lie that 150 million Islamic fundamentalists are members of a peaceful religion. To the contrary, theirs is a deadly religion. Each of the nineteen terrorists involved in wreaking havoc in New York City, Washington, D.C., and the bucolic field outside Stoneycreek Township, Pennsylvania believed he was on a mission from God.

The questions of why Americans are so hated rage on with the answers rarely emerging in the mainstream media:

Why does our government continue to fund Islamic regimes whose fanatical populations are taught terrorist-breeding ideologies?

Why is America selling billions of dollars in arms to Arab states such as Saudi Arabia that continue unabated in support of the same fundamentalist Islamic ideology that fueled the September 11, 2001 attacks? Such countries continue to turn their backs on refugees from Syria and Iraq, demanding instead that America assume responsibility for them.

Events in the Middle East in the last century have fulfilled more biblical prophecies than any since the time of Jesus Christ. It was the twentieth century that saw World Wars—dress rehearsals for the battle of Armageddon, the rebirth of the nation of Israel, and the reemergence of Arabic culture to a prominence it has not enjoyed since it routed the Crusaders at the beginning of the second millennium AD. The rise of proxy wars has blurred any ability to identify the enemy by its uniform. Iran raced ahead with plans to produce a nuclear weapon. This was to have been thwarted by White House efforts to conclude the Iran deal, but instead the rogue country was awarded with what Israeli Prime Minister Benjamin Netanyahu called "a jackpot, a cash bonanza of hundreds of billions of dollars." It also ended a European oil embargo as well as some financial restrictions on banks in Iran. Even after approving the agreement, Iran's leader the Grand Ayatollah Ali Khamenei released a book calling for the annihilation of Israel. He detailed how that would occur based on what he called, "well-established Islamic principles." Not to be outdone, Al-Qaeda leader Ayman al-Zawahiri called for lone-wolf attacks on Western countries similar to those launched by the Boston Marathon bombers in 2013.

Today, America's secular political engine is on a collision course with those Islamic fundamentalists who have vowed to destroy what they call "the Great Satan," the United States. Some churches today have adherents who believe there is nothing we can do about it. Even some Evangelical church leaders have thrown up their hands in surrender. The belief is that if the destruction of the world as we know it is prophesied in the Bible, all we can do is sit back and let disaster strike. That is untrue; prophecy is revealed so that we can take the actions necessary to ensure that the future is one of hope for as many as possible.

Jeremiah 29:11 encourages the Believer with these words, "For I know the thoughts that I think toward you, says the LORD, thoughts of peace and not of evil, to give you a future and a hope." It is time to challenge the lies of the Enemy and say unequivocally, "Satan, you can't have my country, America!"

God-fearing Americans who are willing to step out and make a difference to keep our country headed in the right direction, whether that be in our domestic policy or our foreign policy, must stand up and be counted. We need to do everything in our power to see that our government leaders act with moral clarity on every issue.

In 1981, I was invited to a high-level briefing of U.S. generals and admirals over the sale of AWAC planes to Saudi Arabia. The day before, I had to fly to Virginia Beach. On that flight, I was praying that God would give me insight.

I wrote my prayer on a piece of paper along with the acronym AWAC. The man seated me next to me asked why I had written that. I replied, "I just asked God if He would allow me to meet with the AWAC crew that was in the air when Israel attacked Iraq's nuclear reactor. He looked at me in surprise and said, "I am a member of that crew and we are sitting around you on this plane." The man was unable to respond to my questions regarding that flight, but simply slightly nodded his head yes or no. My first question was: Did you see the Israelis crossing into Iraq? (He nodded yes.) Secondly, did you tell the Saudis? (He nodded no.) Needless to say, when I arrived at the White House I had great insight into what was happening.

I challenged the White House over the decision, stating that those planes might eventually end up in the hands of Islamic fundamentalists and pose a major threat to U.S. and Israeli security. My arguments were mostly pragmatic, but I had so much intelligence information that they let me speak. When I inserted a scripture into my short speech, I was opposed with this question, "What does God know about foreign policy?"

We have to look no further than Psalm 2:6-10 (LB) for the answer to that impertinent question:

> For the Lord declares, "This is the King of my choice, and I have enthroned him in Jerusalem, my holy city." His chosen one replies, "I will reveal the everlasting purposes of God, for the Lord has said to me, 'You are my Son. This is your Coronation Day. Today I am giving you

your glory.' Only ask and I will give you all the nations of the world. Rule them with an iron rod; smash them like clay pots!" O kings and rulers of the earth, listen while there is time. Serve the Lord with reverent fear; rejoice with trembling. Fall down before his Son and kiss his feet before his anger is roused and you perish. I am warning you—his wrath will soon begin. But oh, the joys of those who put their trust in him!

When Ronald Reagan became president, I was invited to be part of a small U.S. delegation to have lunch with him and his Cabinet. Chuck Colson was sitting next to me. It was his first time back in the White House since the Nixon days. I said to Mr. Colson, "I imagine you're thinking all about the White House strategy that's going on in this room." He smiled and said, "Not at all. I'm only thinking about eternity! Tonight I go to death row to share Christ with some inmates. That's what is on my mind. At this season in my life, I am more interested in prayer than politics."

Sooner or later everyone on the planet—rich or poor; skeptic or religious; president or pauper—will be thinking of that one thing . . . eternity. Do we really believe that we can plan the future of our nation—of our world—without considering eternity as well? While democracy may have been conceived in Greece, it was not until Bible-quoting, God-fearing colonists came together to form the United States of America that it has risen to the ideal we know today. Our system may not be perfect, but it is the best our world has seen because it was one established with moral clarity and biblical wisdom.

Join with me as we consider the depths of God's eternal Word in a search for His purpose and plan in the midst of worldwide chaos. As Dr. Martin Luther King Jr. said, "Nothing in the world is more dangerous than sincere ignorance and conscientious stupidity."[17] The United States charged into the 21st century with a terminal case of both.

The first question to be addressed is, "What does God know about your future, my future, and that of the U.S.?" The Bible has much to say about future events.

The struggle we see in the Middle East and the one quickly spreading worldwide began with Ishmael and Isaac, and will end with the descendants of the two sons of Abraham. The ancient brothers gave birth to the two spirits battling for supremacy through their descendants.

Ishmael was not the son of promise, but the son of a man trying to work the will of God in his own way. It was her desperation at being barren that propelled Sarai to offer Hagar, her Egyptian handmaiden, to Abram as a surrogate. Yet, despite Sarai's interference, there is a lesson to be learned. In her misery, she turned from faith in God, from dependence on Jehovah, to works—reliance on Self. She had a plan and nothing was going to deter her from seeing it come to fruition. Hagar represents works—man or, in this instance, woman—taking matters into their own hands. Abram could have said, "No." He could have reminded Sarai that God had made a promise to him and he would continue to believe God. That didn't happen. When presented with a pretty little doe-eyed handmaiden, Abram capitulated. The result: Ishmael.

Though a man of faith, Abraham acted in his own wisdom and lust, not following God's plan; he justified a foolish action through moral relativism, tradition, and human reasoning. He was attempting to gain God's blessing without faith in the Creator. It was some years later when the son of promise, Isaac, was born that Abraham fully realized the gravity of his mistake. Rejecting the "son of human reasoning," God blessed Isaac, the "son of faith."

Ishmael became the father of the Arab race, and Isaac a patriarch of the Hebrews.

Today America is caught in the same kind of battle—the attempt to be effective without reliance upon God, making our halls of government secular, amoral, and hostile to religion. Instead of looking to God for blessings and prosperity, we look to our own reasoning and logic. Our government leaders seem to be willing to abide almost anything to achieve their politically correct goals and agendas. The enemy, in the eyes of these liberal politicians, is the narrow-minded, right-wing, Bible-thumping conservative who believes in black and white, right and wrong. They call such people bigots, yet are willing to overlook real bigotry in other areas to keep their schemes and programs moving forward—no matter the cost.

America knows that the modern-day Ishmael, the older brother in this struggle, still believes the lies Hitler invoked to twist the minds of the Germans: that the Jews were responsible for the ills of the world and especially those of the Arabs; that if they were simply annihilated, the whole world would sleep easier. That same dogma is rampant in Arab countries, yet America does nothing to counteract this vile doctrine. Instead we honor those who preach the same things by calling them "diplomats"—terrorist organizations such as the PLO, HAMAS, Hezbollah, Islamic Jihad, ISIL and others. Then, through negotiations today's Isaac is forced to make more concessions to the implacably angry offspring of Ishmael. However, Ishmael will never be appeased with a Palestinian state; that is only a hoped-for first step. Jihadist organizations use the obliging Palestinians, wave the PA flag and cry "Death to Americans" to capture the minds of the liberal media. We cannot actually believe that they will suddenly love us if Palestine becomes a state.

The Palestinian Authority doesn't want a divided Jerusalem, but instead covets all of it. They do not simply desire to occupy the West Bank, but all of Israel from the Jordan River to the Mediterranean Sea. It is not a matter of "land for peace"; it is a matter of using any means possible to rid the Middle East of the Jewish population altogether, thereby negating any U.S. involvement. They do not wish the subjugation of the Jewish people; they wish their destruction. It is the agenda of such leaders as Palestinian Authority head Mahmoud Abbas and Bashar al-Assad of Syria, as well as the current leaders in Iran.

There is a battle for America that has never been fought, and must be waged. It is a spirit battle! On a thirty-seven acre piece of property in Jerusalem, the temple mount, stands a mosque—the Mosque of Omar. The temple mount is the site where Satan challenged God Almighty with the words:

> For you have said in your heart: I will ascend into heaven, I will exalt my throne above the stars of God; I will also sit on the mount of the congregation On the farthest sides of the north. (Isaiah 14:13, NKJV)

It is thought that the southeast corner of the wall surrounding the Temple Mount was the pinnacle as described in Luke 4, the chapter outlining the temptation of Christ:

> Then he [Satan] brought Him to Jerusalem, set Him on the pinnacle of the temple, and said to Him, "If You are the Son of God, throw Yourself down from here. For it is written: 'He shall give His angels charge over you, To keep you,' and, 'In their hands they shall bear you up, Lest you dash your foot against a stone.'" And Jesus answered and said to him, "It has

been said, 'You shall not tempt the Lord your God.'" (Luke 4:9–12 NKJV)

In Arabic on the walls of the gold-crowned Dome of the Rock on the temple mount are the words:

> O People of the Book! Do not exaggerate in your religion nor utter aught concerning God save the truth. The Messiah, Jesus son of Mary, was only a Messenger of God, and His Word which He conveyed unto Mary, and a spirit from Him. So believe in God and His messengers, and say not 'Three'—Cease! (it is) better for you!—God is only One God.[18]

Recently, in the al Aqsa Mosque also on the temple mount a mullah declared,

> "Muslims are going to be exterminated by the Jews in the end of days. Jews are going to rebuild the temple and worship the devil. The Quran prophesied that trees and rocks will cry out telling Muslims to kill Jews, 'They are hiding behind you.' The Children of Israel will all be exterminated, the Anti-Christ will be killed and the Muslims will live in comfort for a

long time." Jews slaughter gentile children and
drain their blood for use in Passover matzah.
They kidnap a small child, bring a barrel filled
with nails, put the child on the barrel. Their
little body is pierced by nails and in the bottom
of the barrel is a faucet where they drain the
blood.[19]

The result of this demon-possessed rhetoric from
mosques, madrassas and mullahs has been a plague of
Palestinian children stabbing Israelis in the streets. ISIS
admitted blowing up a Russian plane in the Sinai, and is
also very active in Syria—two countries that border Israel.
The stabbings were incited in part by radical Islamic cleric
Sheik Khaled Al-Mughrabi who broadcast lies that Israel
planned to take over control of the temple mount. Such
bombastic outcries only serve to stir up more animosity
for both Israel and the United States. Is it any wonder
that ISIS has called for a plague of suicide bombers in its
"Project Behead Jews?"

It's not only critical that we understand why they hate
us, it is absolutely vital that we understand why they act
on that hatred. The *shahids* believe they are performing a
holy ritual for Allah. From childhood, Muslims are taught

that to be a *shahid*—a martyr—one must be chosen by Allah. It is the greatest honor in life.

Shahids are taught that a martyr does not receive a funeral, but rather a wedding. This is the reason Muslim families do not hold funerals when a child commits an act of martyrdom. Instead, a wedding celebration is held.

The prospective *shahid is* told that when the holy and religious act is performed:

- ✧ He will feel no pain or fear; the sting of death is removed.

- ✧ He will not die; the soul of the *shahid* goes directly to paradise.

- ✧ He will be honored when he arrives in paradise with a crown of glory bearing a jewel signifying the wealth of the world in the center of it. (In Christianity, the crown is placed on the head of Jesus, and the saints lay their crowns at His feet.)

- ✧ He will attend his own wedding with seventy-two black-eyed virgins. The word "black-eyed" does not denote eye color; it denotes that they are incorruptible—an interesting word. This belief is so strong that before the act of martyrdom, the *shahid* shaves all pubic hair, and tapes his private parts. This is symbolic of what is to come.

✧ He will pave the way for seventy relatives to go to paradise, and be exempt from the horrors of hell. In essence, the blood of the *shahid* atones for sin. It certainly would make for a horrible childhood when all of your relatives are lobbying to claim a spot on your "paradise list." The insane aspect of this is that this diabolical battle for the minds of the children begins in kindergarten. Cartoon characters similar to our Mickey Mouse or Donald Duck are employed with a message incorporated to seduce and recruit these small children as *shahids*. Kindergarten camps teach the principles of *jihad*. Bridges, roads, parks and buildings are named after the martyrs. Posters with photos of the martyrs are everywhere.

As I mentioned earlier, on November 13, 2015 a group of shahids struck in Paris. According to the *New York Times*:

> Most of the 129 confirmed fatalities resulted from the mass shooting at a rock concert in the center of the city around 9:20 p.m. local time. Other deaths came after suicide bombings and shootings around the same time in five other locations, including restaurants and a soccer stadium. More than 350 people were wounded, at least 99 of them in critical condition, Paris officials say.... The police made a number of arrests in Brussels [Belgium] on Saturday in connection with the attacks. A Greek official said that a Syrian passport used by a migrant who passed through Greece was found on an assailant's body.[20]

Europe has been flooded with a mass of Muslim Syrian refugees trying to enter various countries to escape slaughter by President Bashar al Assad. Unfortunately, among those who desperately needed sanctuary, including many Assyrian Christians, were those radical Islamists who took advantage of the chaos to slip in undetected in order to attack the unsuspecting. President Obama has declared that the U.S. needs to be more humanitarian and accept a large number of refugees from a terrorist state. Syria and its partner in crime, Iran, have fueled and funded terror for decades, allowing terrorists to establish businesses and become "respectable." Now in Syria, terrorists are killing terrorists. Groups such as Lebanon's Hezbollah, Iran's Revolutionary Guard and ISIS battle each other. Sadly, innocent bystanders also suffer. Christianity has virtually been wiped out in Iraq and Syria by radical Islam, yet no one cries for those Christians who are dispossessed.

Today's war on terrorism is fueled by stone-age hatred—the same hatred Cain had for Abel, Ishmael for Isaac, and Satan for Jesus. Terrorists wage a spiritual war of fear and bigotry beyond anything we can comprehend—such a war cannot be won with tactical weaponry alone. There has never been a more urgent time for American Christians to act with moral clarity than today, yet there has also never been a time in which we have seemed more complacent. The future of our nation, as well as our world, hangs in the balance between our actions and our apathy. Eternity is calling us to do the right thing, and to do it now; not to sit on the sideline and clap our hands as the two sides of Armageddon go through their pre-game warm-ups.

Though William Butler Yeats was not a Christian prophet, I have found few more concise descriptions of the tensions of our times:

> Mere anarchy is loosed upon the world,
> The blood-dimmed tide is loosed, and everywhere
> The ceremony of innocence is drowned;
> The best lack all conviction, while the worst
> Are full of passionate intensity.
> Surely some revelation is at hand;
> Surely the Second Coming is at hand. . .
> somewhere in the sands of the desert
> A shape with lion body and the head of a man,. . .
> And what rough beast, its hour come round at last,
> Slouches towards Bethlehem to be born?[21]

The beast—Satan's right-hand-man, the Antichrist will soon be on the move. The Bible declares that the final battle will take place in Israel, and over Jerusalem. Could it be that the battle lines are already being drawn, that nations are now aligning themselves for the events to come? This seems even more possible with Russian troops now in Syria on the pretext of battling Islamic State jihadists. On which side of the line drawn in the sand will the United States stand? Though Palestinians have been offered their own country time and again—first in 1947 by the United Nations, again in 1991 at the Madrid Conference after the Gulf War, then in 1998 at the Wye River talks, in a desperate President Bill Clinton's final days in office, and the Quartet ascribed to by President George W. Bush. The major stumbling block on the way to peace has always been the question of who controls East Jerusalem, the historic city of David where the Temple Mount rests—the very spot where heaven and earth met, and will meet again. It is there that God has chosen to place His name. (See II Chronicles 6:6)

The United States of America is mired in complacency on such issues, though we have already had countless warnings. While history records various reasons why wars are fought, none go far enough in mentioning the root cause—hatred and bigotry. Many say Hitler could have won the war if he had pressed on to conquer England and left the Russian invasion for warmer times. Such statements overlook the hatred that was the real driving force behind Hitler's war: there were millions of Jews in Russia, few in England.

This spirit of hatred always begins in the same way: it starts with Jew-hatred and then moves on to loathing Christians (between the Nazis and the Soviets, roughly 6 million Christians were martyred during WWII, though not in death camps as the Jews were[22]). Jews were slaughtered simply for being Jewish. Today we see the same hatred exhibited by extreme Islamic Fundamentalists who carry out demonic acts of terror. Many Islamic newspapers are eerily reminiscent of those from the early years of Nazi Germany. Hitler's gospel is back. The truth is: Satan is out to destroy our country; we must stand and fight the good fight of faith against his wiles!

America can ill-afford to ignore the first sign that another world war might soon be upon us: the increase of rabid anti-Semitism in the Arab world and now quickly returning to Europe. How long before we see signs in the United States of unbridled Jew-hatred? Let me ask you a simple question: If America were to routinely begin experiencing suicide attacks in our malls, movie theaters, restaurants, and even churches and synagogues, would it not be better to declare all-out war on hatred and bigotry now?

As Yale Professor David Gelernter wrote in *The Wall Street Journal*:

> Terrorists evidently control large segments of Arab opinion the way the Nazis once controlled Germany—by swagger and lies, by dispensing a dangerous hallucinogenic ideology for the masses, and by murdering opponents.[23]

Why is the U.S. funding anti-Semitic terrorist-harboring regimes? Have we learned nothing from 9-11? Have we forgotten the mobs dancing in the streets of Palestine and the people of other Arab nations screaming "Death to America?" The goal of an Arab conquest of Israel is for another Holocaust, and do not be so naïve as to think Christians will be excluded. Islamic extremists detest everything about America—its emancipation of women, its freedom, its wealth, its power, and its culture. They want to kill Americans because of all we represent—our God allows us things that theirs does not. To them, it is a battle of two books—the Bible and the Qur'an. While liberals in America will tell you we all worship the same God, you won't find any members of *al Qaeda*, Islamic State, or any other such group preaching the same thing. In the Islamic culture an infidel is worthy of death—whether Jew or Christian. If we don't get to the root of it, that rage is going to destroy us.

There is absolutely no question that on God's scale, America has been weighed in the balance and found wanting. The graveyard of history testifies that God rejects nations which reject Him and His Word. Is God getting ready to reject us once and for all?

America's fate will be determined in a final test. It is time to REPENT! It is time to stand toe-to-toe with Satan and shout, "You can't have my country!"

PRAYER FOR AMERICA:

God be merciful to America; bless us, and cause Your face to shine upon her, that Your way may be known on earth, and Your salvation among all nations.

Let the peoples praise You, O God; Let all the peoples praise You. Oh, let the nations be glad and sing for joy! For You shall judge the people righteously, and govern the nations on earth. Let the peoples praise You, O God; let all the peoples praise You. Then the earth will yield her increase; and God, our own God, shall bless us. He shall bless us, and all the ends of the earth shall fear Him. (Psalm 67)

SCRIPTURES FOR STUDY:

Psalm 67	Scriptures for Study:
Joshua 1:3-9	I Chronicles 28:20
Psalm 27:1	Psalm 56: 3-4
Isaiah 41:10	Isaiah 41:13
Isaiah54:4	Romans 8:15
II Timothy 1:7	Hebrews 13:5-6

5

AMERICA AND PROPHECY

Now learn this parable from the fig tree:
When its branch has already become tender,
and puts forth leaves, you know that summer
is near. So you also, when you see these things
happening, know that it is near—at the doors!

MARK 13:28-29, NKJV

THE RIVER OF PROPHECY is filled with rapids, obstacles, eddies, and undercurrents. How can the Believer navigate them prayerfully and successfully? It often has more to do with milestones we see along the way than in the details of how something foretold comes to fruition. Events tend to swirl in the currents as prophecy moves towards fulfillment. Sometimes it seems to move ahead briskly, other times coming to an abrupt halt. It flows backwards for a time as its energy builds, or even disappears from sight only to reemerge further downstream. This often makes finding where we are in prophecy confusing if you look merely at the currents. It is often difficult to determine what progress has been made downstream unless it is gauged in relation to the bank. This is why God gave us mile markers along the way to alert us to what is coming next. Thus if we look at where we have come from, it can be easier to see how to handle the rapids and undertows in the river of prophecy. By understanding the flow of the last few centuries, and seeing how those events relate to the pattern of events occurring today, we begin to clearly see what Bible prophecy holds for America.

America today is still regarded as a world leader, and the keys to her future are not buried in some biblical code, but in understanding the will of God as He prepares for the final battle that will usher in the millennial reign of Christ.

Many look at prophecy and think that because certain things are ordained to come to pass, it gives us reason to sit back and wait. I disagree. As in the days of Noah, many continue to eat and drink, marry and be given in marriage, and yet disaster—or deliverance—is at the door. Which one will be allowed to enter is clearly up to you and me.

While many may think the fulfillment of biblical prophecy is a sovereign act of God, the scriptures themselves indicate something quite different. When God was about to destroy Sodom and Gomorrah, He asked the rhetorical question, "Shall I hide from Abraham that thing which I do?" (Genesis 18:17) God felt He should take no action of judgment without granting His friend Abraham the right to intercede on behalf of the two evil cities.

As Daniel was reading in the Book of Jeremiah, he came across a scripture that said, "After seventy years be accomplished at Babylon I will visit you, and perform my good word toward you, in causing you to return to this place." (Jeremiah 29:10) Daniel did some quick calculations—over seventy years had already passed and Israel was still in captivity under Babylon! So he began to pray God's promise back to Him. Thus the heart of Babylonian King Cyrus was softened and Nehemiah was given permission to rebuild Jerusalem and the temple.

As Jesus said:

> You are my friends if you do what I command. I no longer call you servants, because a servant *does not know* his master's business. Instead, I have called you friends, *for everything that I learned from my Father I have made known to you.* (John 15:14-15 NIV [emphasis added])

As Jesus' friends, we should know what He is planning concerning events for our nation. We should be involved in prayer. As it was with Daniel, God yearns for someone to agree with Him, pray His promises into reality, and carry out His plan on Earth.

In the parable of the Fig Tree (Matthew 24:32-44), Jesus told his disciples that when we begin to see the events He foretold earlier in that chapter, they would be indications of the end of this age—just as new leaves on the fig tree would indicate that summer was coming—and that the generation that saw these things would also see end-time prophecy fulfilled. Look for a moment at what Jesus said would mark the final age and His return:

Many apostates would come in His name.
(Matthew 24:5, 11)

Jesus said, "I am the way, the truth, and the life. No one comes to the Father except through Me." (John 14:6 NKJV)

And you shall know the truth, and the truth shall make you free. (John 8:32, NKJV)

There would be wars and rumors of wars.
(Matthew 24:6-7)

Jesus said, "Peace I leave with you,
My peace I give to you; not as the world gives do
I give to you. Let not your heart be troubled,
neither let it be afraid." (John 14:27, NKJV)

There will be famines, epidemic diseases,
and earthquakes. (Matthew 24:7)

Safety and salvation come from God alone:

Then the Lord said to Noah, "Come into the ark,
you and all your household, because I have seen
that you *are* righteous before Me in this generation." (Genesis 7:1) Then in an act of protection
and redemption, God shut the door behind Noah
and his family. (Verse 16)

Persecution shall increase. (Matthew 24:8-10)

Because you have made the Lord, *who is* my refuge,
Even the Most High, your dwelling place,
No evil shall befall you, Nor shall any plague

come near your dwelling;
For He shall give His angels charge over you,
To keep you in all your ways.
In *their* hands they shall bear you up,
Lest you dash your foot against a stone.
(Psalm 91:9-12, NKJV)

Sin shall flourish and Christian loves
will grow cold. (Matthew 24:12)

"But you, dear friends, must build up your lives
ever more strongly upon the foundation
of our holy faith, learning to pray in the power
and strength of the Holy Spirit. Stay always
within the boundaries where God's love
can reach and bless you."
(Jude 1:20-21a, LB)

While there are other signs of the end-times foretold in the Bible, these are sufficient for us to realize that the season of which Jesus spoke is upon us. While we don't know the exact day or hour, the leaves of the fig tree definitely have sprouted and are flourishing. It is time that we understood the significance of today's events and our nation's precarious position between the two sons of Abraham, so that we know what to do in the days to come.

Since the destruction of the temple and Jerusalem by the Romans in ad 70, the single most significant event of prophecy has been the reunification of the nation of Israel on May 14, 1948. This places us on the doorstep of three events: 1) the Rapture, 2) the seven-year peace treaty between the Antichrist and the nation of Israel that marks the beginning of the Tribulation, and 3) the rebuilding of the Temple in Jerusalem. While scholars disagree on the order in which these will happen, it is clear that they will probably all occur within a short period of time—a span of only a few years. If we are reading the signs of the times correctly, they are likely to happen soon, probably within our generation. Jesus said, "When you see all these things, know that it is near—at the doors! . . . This generation will by no means pass away till all these things take place," (Matthew 24:33-34 njkv) It is extremely likely that the current events reported in the Middle East are setting the stage for what will happen in the world during the Tribulation.

There are many things on the prophecy timeline that apply uniquely to Israel as prophecy's timeclock. The spirit of Antichrist that has become so active in the last century is, not surprisingly, rabidly anti-Semitic. While the twentieth century was the most horrendous period of Christian persecution in the history of the world, it was also the time of the Holocaust in Eastern Europe and the pogroms designed to rid Russia of Jews. Today the greatest persecution of Christians occurs in fundamentalist Muslim countries under *Shari'a* Law (the religious criminal code set forth in the Qur'an), whose news media are also filled with disdain for the Jews. These are the white-hot embers that keep the fires of anti-Semitism and terrorism ablaze.

This "spirit of Antichrist" has been behind the greatest threats to freedom we have seen in the last century: fascism, Nazism, communism, and now Wahhabism—the form of fundamentalist Islam that fuels terrorist rage. If we read trends correctly, it is also the spirit behind much of liberalism's secular relativism that is now attempting to silence God's voice in America. Though this spirit has also infected blocs of the church from time to time to turn it toward apostasy (as it seems to be doing today) and anti-Semitism (as it has done often in the past), we should not be confused by this seeming crossover. II Thessalonians 2:7, ESV, states clearly, "Only he who now restrains it [total lawlessness] will do so until he is out of the way." That "one" mentioned in scripture is the body of Christ on earth—the Church. The moment Christ comes for His Christ, this old world will be in big trouble.

The true Church will always follow the Spirit of Christ, exhibiting His true fruit and gifts, not those who have turned toward political correctness rather than allowing the love of God to rule. Should the U.S. cut her ties with Jerusalem—continuing down the road of moral relativism that seems to have drugged the State Department and liberals in the U.S.—it is easy to foresee how we could surely be a nation on the cusp of destruction. Why is that important to the Believer? In Genesis 12:3, NKJV, we read these sobering words, "I will bless those who bless you, And I will curse him who curses you; And in you all the families of the earth shall be blessed."

However, rather than turn her back on Israel, I believe America is presented with another course. As the Bible says, "Blessed is the nation whose God is the Lord," (Psalm 33:12 NKJV) and "Righteousness exalts a nation, but sin is a disgrace." (Proverbs 14:34 NKJV)

Politics and the course of our nation do not determine what is in our hearts; it is a *result* of what is there. If God is to truly heal our land, it is not just a question of correct foreign and domestic policy, but an issue of the Church of the United States rejecting relativism and earnestly seeking God and His ways above all else. Our battle is not a conflict between Christian and secular *culture*, but between good and evil, between the Spirit of Christ and the spirit of Antichrist, between revealing Jesus to our world and being satisfied with complacency and lukewarm spirituality. America's roots were firmly established in the moral clarity of the Bible and prayer. If we call on God to heal our land, America will avoid being swallowed up in the spirit of the world that will put us on the wrong side in the battle of Armageddon.

Whether or not the Rapture takes place tomorrow or not for many years, there are things we can do to assure peace in our time. With the help of God we can accomplish what no other nation on earth could ever hope to do, but we can't do it without a major course correction. It is time to realign our moral compass. The Church needs to be a purpose-driven body of Believers, determined to preach the truth from the pulpits in America, determined to be salt and light to a dark and hopeless world.

Sadly, too many pastors today have bought into the

SPECIAL FREE OFFER*

We trust you are enjoying this book by *New York Times* #1 Best Selling author, Dr. Mike Evans.

Dr. Evans has written a second book in this series entitled, *Satan, You Can't Have Israel*. Mike Evans is one of America's top experts on Israel. He is the founder of the Jerusalem Prayer Team (jerusalemprayerteam.org), and the Friends of Zion Heritage Center and Museum (FOZmuseum.com) in Jerusalem.

From the time of Abraham, God was clear in His promise: "I will bless them that bless thee, and curse him that curseth thee..." Genesis 12:3. In this new, informative and inspirational book, Dr. Evans explains that no weapon formed against the tiny nation of Israel is more powerful than the

will and courage of you, the God-fearing, praying Believer.

Because you have purchased *Satan, You Can't Have my Country*, as a special bonus you may request one copy of Dr. Mike Evans' new 160 page book, *Satan, You Can't Have Israel* and pay only the postage and packaging fee of $5.00.

PLEASE RETURN
THIS CARD WITH $5

(TO COVER POSTAGE AND PACKAGING)

MAIL TO:

ATTN: Mike Evans
TimeWorthy Books
P. O. Box 30000
Phoenix, AZ 85046-0009

OR RESPOND ONLINE AT:

www.SatanBackOff.com

THIS OFFER IS GOOD ONLY IN THE U.S.

Name

Street Address

State   Zip

PLEASE CHARGE $5 TO MY BANK CARD

CC #

Expiration Date

Signature

worldview that the Church is just another social venue. According to author and researcher George Barna:

> The research shows that when pastors evaluate the success of their church, they measure attendance, dollars raised, number of staff, number of programs and square footage. All of those are logical measures to explore. The only problem is that Jesus did not die a horrible and unjust death on the cross to fill sanctuaries, generate cash, populate programs, hire religious professionals or build out campuses.[24]

We stand as Nineveh did when receiving the message of Jonah—we have the choice of either continuing as we have leaving God behind, or repenting and experiencing revival. We are at a crossroads, but more significantly, we are in the crosshairs of those who hate Christians and all for which the United States stands. To these we must respond both spiritually and naturally, with Christian love and compassion and political wisdom based on clarity of vision and moral integrity. It is a worthy calling far more powerful than the call to martyrdom for jihadist suicide bombers. Yet until we live with greater conviction than they die with, our generation will experience nothing of what God wishes for us.

Had the Church obeyed the Great Commission to be a witness unto Him in Jerusalem, Judea and Samaria, Islamic fundamentalists such as Hamas would not have been able to corrupt the minds of children with hatred for Jews and Christians. Instead, those children would have been exposed to a Christianity filled with love. The truth is: Palestinian Christians do not blow up Jews. Revival would be spreading across the Middle East, and the tragic events of 9-11 might never have happened.

Did the Church fail this nation, and our Lord? Is the Church guilty in the eyes of God? Is it too late? No, it's not; but if ever the Church of Jesus Christ plans to repent and follow the Great Commission, rather than continuing to pursue the "Great Omission", it is now!

I pray that pastors will again preach on the Second Coming of the Lord and on Hell. The fiery protestant preacher, Jonathan Edwards, was the acknowledged leader of the First Great Awakening. He had emerged from both Puritan and Calvinist origins but stressed the spiritual necessity of a personal relationship with Christ. Edwards was described as "solemn, with a distinct and careful enunciation, and a slow cadence."[25] Even so, he was known for his authoritative sermons. One of his most well-known was the classic "Sinners in the Hands of an Angry God." So powerful were the word images created by Edwards that people could be heard crying out during his sermon, "What shall I do to be saved?"

There never was a time in history when God dwelt in a Church with an earthly perspective. It is time to proclaim this message. Why? Because the world has taken over the Church. Abortion, divorce, pornography, drugs, alcohol and even homosexuality are alive and well in today's Church. Many pastors allow fear of retaliation to keep them from preaching against these matters.

As a minister of the Gospel, God has placed one message on my heart to preach in this hour: Jesus is coming! The Bible says, "I know your deeds, that you are neither cold nor hot. I wish you were either one or the other! So, because you are lukewarm—neither hot nor cold—I am about to spit you out of my mouth."

The Shepherd is calling for spiritual warriors—will you answer His call? If so, we need to understand the currents of American prophecy so that we know how to navigate the waters that lie ahead.

PRAYER FOR AMERICA:

Father,

Your Word says that no weapon formed against me shall prosper. I stand on that promise for America. You also tell me that I dwell in the secret place of the Most High, under the shadow of the Almighty. Lord, I acknowledge You in all my ways so that You strengthen me for warfare through the power of the Holy Spirit. You have promised never to leave me or forsake me. The Psalmist David said, "For Jehovah is my refuge! I choose the God above all gods to shelter me." (Psalm 91:9, LB)

SCRIPTURES FOR STUDY:

Psalm 4:8   Psalm 91:1-16

Psalm 28:7   Ezra 8:21

II Timothy 4:18   Matthew 28:20

Psalm 37:39-40   Proverbs 1:33

Proverbs 29:25   Job 28:28

6

PRINCIPALITIES, POWERS & PRAYER:
JUDAH AND THE ROMAN EMPIRE

For we wrestle not against flesh and blood,
but against principalities, against powers,
against the rulers of the darkness of this world,
against spiritual wickedness in high places.

EPHESIANS 6:12, KJV

MANY EQUATE the present-day state of affairs in the United States with those of the Roman Empire just before its fall. So great was the fall that it took Edward Gibbon, a British historian, six volumes to express its causes and resulting consequences. Like the wise man who built his house on the sand, "And great was the fall of it." (Matthew 7:27, KJV)

Pastor C. D. Harriger wrote of the reasons for the fall:

> Corrupting trends such as unchecked greed,
> increased divorce rates, breakdown of the fam-
> ily, rampant immorality, the unholy desire for
> pleasure and violent entertainment, increased
> taxation... are factors that brought on the demise
> of the empire.[26]

In 2007, editor-at-large Cullen Murphy of *Vanity Fair* wrote *Are We Rome?* He outlines several parallels between the two entities, one being how Americans view their country. Murphy said:

> Rome prized its status as the city around which
> the world revolved. Official Washington shares
> that Ptolemaic outlook. Unfortunately, it is not
> a self-fulfilling prophecy—just a faulty premise.
> And it leads to an exaggerated sense... of its
> importance in the eyes of others, and of its
> ability to act alone.[27]

One needs only to watch CNN or Fox to see how great the divide is. The two prevailing political parties in the United States are unable to work together for the common good of the people who elected the Congressmen to office.

The ruling republic in Rome—the aristocrats (*Optimates*) and the populists (*Populares*)—failed to unite, thus leading to the rise of the dictator Caesar, and the collapse of the Roman Empire. Washington exudes that same lack of harmony. There are some politicos, wise men and women, who strive to bring accord back to the halls of Congress, but it is an uphill battle.

At one time, the President of the United States was widely acknowledged to be the leader of the free world; that is no longer as generally accepted as it once was. Robert Spencer, journalist with *Frontpage Magazine*, wrote in 2013:

> When even the *New York Times* admits that Barack Obama has been outfoxed, outsmarted and outplayed [by Vladimir Putin], you know he has *really* been outfoxed, outsmarted and outplayed.[28]

The U.S. belief in its own technology and military might is sadly misplaced in today's world. At one time the U.S. possessed the only atomic capabilities worldwide; that designation is now shared by Israel, Russia, the United Kingdom, France, China, India, Pakistan and North Korea.

The dominance of the U.S., once taken for granted, exists no longer.

Sadly, politicians in the Roman Empire were corrupt. Can the same be said of many U.S. members of Congress? A long list of public servants in the nation's capital have, over the years, been charged with a variety of crimes, including drug possession, fraud, witness tampering, perjury and sex scandals. Among those were Vice President Spiro Agnew, President William J. "Bill" Clinton (impeached by the House, acquitted by the Senate), Ted Kennedy, John Mitchell, John Dean, Charles "Chuck" Colson, and others implicated in the Watergate Scandal. President Richard M. Nixon resigned to escape charges being brought against him.

In the Roman Empire, it was almost inevitable that politicians lined their pockets at the expense of the common man. Men vied for office as a means of obtaining wealth. Those in power rebuffed every attempt to halt any suggested reforms. The political corruption hastened the demise of the Republic. Many, dare I say most of the politicians walking today's halls of Congress have regressed to having one major goal:

Their focus is therefore not so much on the people who sent them to Washington. Their focus is instead on those who will make them rich in Washington.[29]

Another cause thought to have contributed to its fall was Rome's involvement in wars with the Italians, Greeks, Carthaginians, and Macedonians, to name but a few of its foes. The list of wars in which the U.S. has been engaged is equally long: two World Wars, the Korean Conflict, the Vietnam War, the Cold War, Operation Desert Storm, Operation Iraqi Freedom, the war in Afghanistan, and the ongoing war against terrorism. This focus on war leads predominately to domestic issues taking a lower priority. Families are torn apart; operational funds are spread thin; veterans' needs are too often overlooked or poorly met, the nation loses far too many young men and women as a result of these conflicts, and the economy suffers. There are those economists who believe that the economic advantage is shifting to China, India and perhaps even to Brazil. The move to China has already caused perilous stock market fluctuations in recent years.

The story is told of Benjamin Franklin and an encounter

he had with a Mrs. Powel following the Constitutional Convention in 1787. The lady asked, "Well Doctor, what have we got, a republic or a monarchy." Franklin replied, "A republic if you can keep it."[30]

Another comparison can be drawn between the United States and the ancient kingdom of Judah in 7 and 6 BC, after the death of King David and following Solomon's apostasy. Some of the Israelites made a public show of continuing to obey the precepts of God, but it was all about appearances.

The United States is founded on Judeo-Christian principles. Dr. Richard Lee, author and founding pastor of First Redeemer Church in Atlanta wrote:

> America's Founding Fathers gave us the country's founding documents, such as the Declaration of Independence, the Constitution, the Bill of Rights and others. In order for them to form such documents, they had to lean upon some common understanding of law, government, social order and a basic moral code. These understandings sprang from a common acceptance of what has come to be known as the Judeo-Christian Ethic. The term "Judeo-Christian" refers to

"the influence of the Hebrew Bible and the New
Testament on one's system of values, laws and
ethical code." It is not just a system of theologi-
cal thought, but a culture of values as seen in
one's individual's right to life, liberty and the
pursuit of happiness.[31]

Dissenters point out that some of the men who set in
motion the formation of the United States were Deists,
believers in the idea that God created the heavens and
earth, and then retreated, leaving mankind to do his
own thing. That belief, however, did not keep them from
basing the new republic on biblical ideas and ideals. None
of those men present at the signing of the Declaration of
Independence could look down through the corridors of
time and sense that the Supreme Court would one day
step outside these boundaries established by the founding
fathers. Those jurists, instead of simply interpreting the
Constitution, now add opinions establishing laws contrary
to those originally intended.

In Judah, the ethical, moral and behavior patterns
showed a total lack of belief in and reliance on Jehovah
God. II Chronicles 3:15-16, LB, makes a clear statement
regarding why Judah was sent into captivity:

Jehovah the God of their fathers sent his prophets again and again to warn them, for he had compassion on his people and on his Temple. But *the people mocked these messengers of God and despised their words*, scoffing at the prophets until the anger of the Lord could no longer be restrained, and there was no longer any remedy. (Emphasis mine.)

It is a succinct picture of how a nation can self-destruct when God and *His* laws are ignored. A loving Jehovah had done all that could possibly be done to warn the people that judgment was coming. Proverbs 29:1, ESV, reminds us:

He who is often reproved, yet stiffens his neck, will suddenly be broken beyond healing. (The King James Version reads, "Without remedy.")

This pattern is being replicated in the United States. Rather than standing firm and strong in their belief in Jehovah God, many are "going with the flow." President John F. Kennedy said, "Conformity is the jailer of freedom and the enemy of growth."[32] Following the crowd can be a deadly exercise.

In his letter to the Romans, the Apostle Paul warned:

> And do not be conformed to this world, but be
> transformed by the renewing of your mind, that
> you may prove what *is* that good and acceptable
> and perfect will of God. (Romans 12:2, NKJV)

Pastors and evangelists who have had the temerity to stand up and issue warnings have often been ridiculed. This has occurred in my life. In 1999, years before the 9-11 attack I released a book, *The Jerusalem Scroll*, which included an attack on the Twin Towers in New York City. I was ridiculed by many for daring to even think in fictional terms of an attack on the continental United States.

This offering was followed by my 2003 bestseller, *Beyond Iraq, The Next Move*, in which I predicted that an Islamic revolution would be birthed in Iraq; that without the power of prayer, the war would leave the world with a marching army of human corpses dispensing plagues. I also stated that the war with radical Islam would not end in Iraq; it would only begin there.

The sequel, *The Final Move Beyond Iraq: The Final Solution While the World Sleeps,* was a #1 *New York Times* bestseller. In that book, I clearly outlined the apocalyptic

Islamic army that would form a caliphate as a result of the Iraq war. Its global ambition to confront the West would wreak havoc in the region and spread its poisonous tentacles even wider. The result was an all-out attack by the Liberal Left on the premise of the book during network television debates and interviews.

Jeremiah 6:16-17, ESV, is a bold call for repentance and return with a sad response:

> Thus says the LORD: "Stand by the roads, and look, and ask for the ancient paths, where the good way is; and walk in it, and find rest for your souls. But they said, 'We will not walk in it.' I set watchmen over you, saying, 'Pay attention to the sound of the trumpet!' But they said, 'We will not pay attention.'"

God brought judgment on those who refused to heed His call. The Rev. Mr. George Whitefield preached a sermon in Glasgow, Scotland on October 22, 1742 titled, "The Great Danger of Conformity to the World." In that homily, he warned:

> The generality of Christians are so blended with the World, are so exceedingly Compliant, so

exceedingly pliable, that one will scarce know who is on God's side and who is on the World's side. We are indeed grown conformists in the worst Sense, not to the Rites and Ceremonies of a Church, but unto the Corruptions of the World.[33]

God has been trying to get the attention of the Church for centuries. It is time Believers heed the message and begin to pray and seek His face for another Great Awakening.

PRAYER FOR AMERICA:

You said "If My people who are called by My name will humble themselves, and pray and seek My face, and turn from their wicked ways, then I will hear from heaven, and will forgive their sin and heal their land." This day, I humble myself in prayer and intercession for America; I seek Your face; I repent of my wicked ways. Father, please heal our land.

SCRIPTURES FOR STUDY:

I Timothy 2:1	Psalm 33:12
Isaiah 60:18	Micah 4:3
Jeremiah 18:6-10	Hosea 2:18
Psalm 67:1-7	Isaiah 60:12
Proverbs 14:34	Psalm 2:8

7

FACING THE CONSEQUENCES
OF OUR CHOICES

Do not be deceived, God is not mocked; for
whatever a man sows, that he will also reap"
(Gal. 6:7). Paul's words form a stark reminder
to us that our choices have consequences. . .

BILL CROWDER, *Our Daily Bread*[34]

THE FOUNDATIONAL PROMISE on which the
return of Jesus Christ and all prophecy is contingent is
found in Matthew 24:14: "This gospel of the kingdom
shall be preached in the whole world as a testimony to all
the nations, and then the end will come." This doctrine is
taught and followed by more than one billion Christians
worldwide who consider themselves Evangelicals.

The Middle East is the last frontier for the proclama-
tion of the Great Commission, fulfilling the final words
of Jesus on earth:

But you will receive power when the Holy Spirit has come upon you; and you shall be My witnesses both in Jerusalem, and in all Judea and Samaria, and even to the remotest part of the earth (Acts 1:8).

Good versus evil is the doctrine of the Bible from Genesis to the cross and to the very end of the age. According to an oft-quoted saying by Irish philosopher Edmund Burke, "All that is required for evil to triumph is for good men to do nothing." It was the same doctrine Ronald Reagan used in defeating the so-called "Evil Empire" of the Soviet Union. Yet, while Americans rejoiced over the breakup of the former Soviet Union, Russian President Vladimir Putin was busily working to resurrect the remains of that once-dead empire. Russian troops invaded parts of the Ukraine in an attempt to re-annex land formerly under Soviet control, and Putin has dispatched troops to Syria to bolster the rule of Bashar al Assad, a Russian proxy.

The challenges issued to the United States by Russia, by ISIL and other terrorist organizations evoke an invitation to return to God or face the consequences of our choices. We must answer the call to wage war against evil.

Why is this necessary for followers of Christ? How is this mission based on the Bible, and how will it birth a Great Awakening in America, causing these Believers to refocus their passions on confronting the root of all evil?

The question is often asked: How can Christians support a war when Jesus has said, "Love your enemies"? The New Testament clearly states that civil magistrates can wage war against "all enemies, both foreign and domestic." In Romans 13:1–4 we read:

> Every person is to be in subjection to the governing authorities For there is no authority except from God, and those which exist are established by God. Therefore whoever resists authority has opposed the ordinance of God; and they who have opposed will receive condemnation upon themselves. For rulers are not a cause of fear for good behavior, but for evil. Do you want to have no fear of authority? Do what is good and you will have praise from the same; for it is a minister of God to you for good. But if you do what is evil, be afraid; for it does not bear the sword for nothing; for it is a minister of God, an avenger who brings wrath on the one who practices evil.

The Liberal Left hates the America of which Christian presidents have long dreamt—that the Bible and Christians, in general, might return to a place of influence. Christians these days are too often subjected to scorn, ridicule, and discrimination. There is no attack on US culture more deadly than the secular humanists' attack against God in American public life.

The insults and verbal abuse are so severe that anyone who contradicts is labeled "ignorant, evil, racist, and bigot." The dumbing-down of America is well under way, and all in the name of political correctness and the new godless globalism.

The hippies of the 60s with their "God is dead" revolution of rebellion and immorality were confronted with eternity with the assassinations of three men: John F. Kennedy, Robert Kennedy and Dr. Martin Luther King, Jr. When humanity is confronted with eternity, there is always a response: rebellion or repentance. Humanity chose rebellion as did those men who built the Tower of Babel (see Genesis 11). It was to be a symbol of their own desire to be equal with God, but Jehovah thwarted their plans and destroyed their arrogant aspirations by confounding their language.

Today, these same men and women of the 1960s whose drug-induced desire was to "become like the gods" have instead become the very establishment against which they once railed. American culture, the media, educational system, courts, arts and sciences, public and private sectors, mainstream Hollywood, public schools, Washington politics, and the judiciary on every level are run by these once-upon-a-time liberals who are self-destructing. America, the noble experiment, is under siege. A tidal wave of evil is sweeping across our nation: the self-injuring, spirit-destroying, conscious-searing practices of pornography, abortion, homosexuality, and drug and alcohol abuse are condoned and supported as they have never been before.

There is a vicious moral and spiritual war raging in the hearts and minds of Americans. At the center of that battle is the reality that over the past several decades, God has slowly been driven from almost every public institution; and it began with the schoolhouse. It has spread to the courthouse, and in recent years, even to the church house! Our coins have come under attack—those that bear the words, "in God we trust"—and the Pledge of Allegiance has come under fire. "Freedom of speech" seems to apply to everyone except the Christian.

At the heart of liberalism is a belief that evil really doesn't exist; people are basically good, and thus individuals can't be held accountable for the wrong they do. The liberal tactic is that it is better just to talk with people, rather than bringing criminals to justice or fighting to stop those committing crimes against humanity.

The Liberal Left crowd wants God and the Bible driven out of America. Our first president, George Washington, said:

> It is impossible to govern the world without God and the Bible. Reason and experience forbid us to expect that morality can prevail in exclusion of religious principle.[35]

President John Adams agreed:

> Our Constitution was made only for a moral and religious people. It is wholly inadequate to the government of any other.[36]

Can the liberal, secular humanists' hatred for all things Christian pass Natan Sharansky's "town square test"?

> Can a person walk into the middle of the town square and express his or her views without fear

of arrest, imprisonment, or physical harm? If he can, then that person is living in a free society. If not, it's a fear society.[37]

The right of a Christian in America to express his or her views without fear of retaliation is frequently challenged and slowly eroding. I believe America is under attack by radical Islam solely because this is a Christian nation. The late President Ronald Reagan delivered a discourse about the threat of evil in the world and the hope of freedom. Reagan quoted John 3:15, KJV, as his favorite verse: "That whosoever believeth in him should not perish, but have eternal life." It was his favorite, he said, because "having accepted Jesus Christ as my Savior, I have God's promise of eternal life in heaven."

Reagan saw the evil of communism not only as shutting down the churches, but as threatening the eternal salvation of millions of people. He said of freedom:

> Above all, we must realize that no arsenal, or no weapon in the arsenals of the world, is so formidable as the will and moral courage of free men and women. It is a weapon our adversaries in today's world do not have.[38]

Mother Teresa and I once met in Rome where she told me she had encountered Mr. Reagan in June 1981 following the assassination attempt on his life. She recalled saying to the president, "You have suffered the passion of the cross and have received grace. There is a purpose to this. Because of your suffering and pain, you will now understand the suffering of the world. This has happened to you at this time because your country and the world need you."

She said Nancy Reagan broke into tears, and Mr. Reagan was deeply moved. Maureen Reagan Revell, the president's daughter, told me that her father repeated the story often, saying, "God has spared me for a reason. I will devote the rest of my time here on earth to find out what He intends me to do."

Mr. Reagan was greatly influenced by the writings of C. S. Lewis, and especially his book *Mere Christianity*, particularly Book 1, which is entitled "Right and Wrong as a Clue to the Meaning of the Universe." The writings of Alexander Solzhenitsyn were also an influence. The Russian historian, author and dissident addressed the Harvard graduating class in 1978 with a speech entitled "A World Split Apart." He characterized the current conflict for our planet as a physical and spiritual war that has already begun and cannot be won without dealing with the forces of evil. His address to the assembly is as relevant today as it was over thirty years ago:

> A decline in courage may be the most striking feature that an outside observer notices in the West today. The Western world has lost its civic courage, both as a whole and separately, in each country, in each government, in each political party, and, of course, in the United Nations. Such a decline in courage is particularly noticeable among the ruling and intellectual elites, causing an impression of a loss of courage by the entire society. There are many courageous individuals, but they have no determining influence on public life.
>
> Political and intellectual functionaries exhibit this depression, passivity, and perplexity in their actions and in their statements, and even more so in their self-serving rationales as to how realistic, reasonable, and intellectually and even morally justified it is to base state policies on weakness and cowardice. And the decline in courage, at times attaining what could be termed a lack of manhood, is ironically emphasized by

occasional outbursts and inflexibility on the
part of those same functionaries when dealing
with weak governments and with countries that
lack support, or with doomed currents which
clearly cannot offer resistance. But they get
tongue-tied and paralyzed when they deal with
powerful governments and threatening forces,
with aggressors and international terrorists.[39]

As I have often said, the real crisis we in the United
States face today is a spiritual one; at its root, it is a test
of moral will and faith. Whittaker Chambers, the man
whose own religious conversion made him a witness to
one of the terrible traumas of our time, the Hiss-Chambers
case, wrote:

The crisis of the Western world exists to the
degree in which it is indifferent to God. It exists
to the degree in which the Western world actually shares Communism's materialist vision, is so
dazzled by the logic of the materialist interpre-
tation of history, politics and economics that it
fails to grasp that, for it, the only possible answer
to the Communist challenge: Faith in God or
Faith in Man? is the challenge: Faith in God.[40]

It was C. S. Lewis who, in his unforgettable *Screwtape Letters*, wrote:

> The greatest evil is not done now in those sordid 'dens of crime' that Dickens loved to paint. . . . It is conceived and ordered; moved, seconded, carried and minuted in clear, carpeted, warmed, and well-lighted offices, by quiet men with white collars and cut fingernails and smooth-shaven cheeks who do not need to raise their voice. . . .[41]

And Ronald Reagan who said:

> So in your discussions of the nuclear freeze proposals I urge you to beware the temptation of pride—the temptation to blithely declare your-selves above it all and label both sides equally at fault, to ignore the facts of history and the aggressive impulses of an evil empire, to simply call the arms race a giant misunderstanding and thereby remove yourself from the struggle between right and wrong and good and evil. . . I believe we shall rise to the challenge. I believe that communism is another sad, bizarre chapter in human history whose last pages have been written. I believe this because the source of our

strength in the quest for human freedom is not material, but spiritual. And because it knows no limitation, it must terrify and ultimately triumph over those who would enslave their fellow man. For in the words of Isaiah, "He giveth power to the faint; and to them that have no might He increased strength. But they that wait upon the Lord shall renew their strength; they shall mount up with wings as eagles; they shall run, and not be weary."[42]

A painting entitled *A Charge to Keep* hung in the Oval Office while it was occupied by George W. Bush. It was inspired by the artist's favorite song by Charles Wesley. There is a determined rider ahead of two other riders urging his horse up a steep, narrow path. Words to Wesley's song include:

> A charge to keep I have,
> a God to glorify,
> a never-dying soul to save,
> and fit it for the sky.
> To serve the present age,
> my calling to fulfill;
> O may it all my powers engage
> to do my Master's will![43]

When He reached the age of twelve, the time had come for Jesus to take His place among the men of the village and participate in the various Jewish observances. As Mary and Joseph prepared for the trek to Jerusalem to observe Passover, Jesus likely joined with friends near His age. The young family enjoyed their stay in Jerusalem, not for the required two days, but for seven days.

At the conclusion of the feast, the family gathered its belongings and joined the crowd returning to Nazareth. After having traveled a full day, the parents suddenly realized Jesus was not in the company of His friends. Apparently He was a trustworthy boy old enough to celebrate His first *bar mitzvah* and therefore His absence had not raised an alarm. Perhaps it was time for dinner when He was missed, and a frantic Mary and Joseph turned their donkey around and began the long journey back to Jerusalem. After three days of fear and anguish, of searching and longing, the parents found Jesus in the Temple court.

It is likely that Jesus stayed behind, not to cause pain to His parents, but from an insatiable desire for knowledge, and maybe for another reason altogether. It could be that the reason is found in Luke 2:48–50:

So when they saw Him, they were amazed; and His mother said to Him, "Son, why have You done this to us? Look, Your father and I have sought You anxiously." And He said to them, "Why did you seek Me? *Did you not know that I must be about My Father's business?"* But they did not understand the statement which He spoke to them. (Emphasis mine)

It is time for the Church to be about the Father's business. What does that involve? James 4:7 says, "Submit yourselves therefore to God. Resist the devil, and he will flee from you." My friend, it's time to stand firm and shout: Satan, you can't have my country!

PRAYER FOR AMERICA:

Father,

I love America. In the Bible You declare, "Call to me and I will answer you and show you great and mighty things which you do not know." (Jeremiah 33:3) I call unto You right now for my beloved nation. I ask You to pour out Your Holy Spirit on America. Bring a Great Awakening rather than a rude awakening. In the mighty name of Jesus, I bind principalities and powers and spiritual wickedness in high places. I declare that Jesus is Lord over America. I pray that the weapons available to me through the power of prayer will be mighty, pulling down the strongholds over America. In Jesus name!

SCRIPTURES FOR STUDY:

Ephesians 3:10   Psalm 122:1

Matthew 16:17   Ephesians 1:22

Hebrews 10:25   Colossians 1:18

Acts 20:28   Acts 12:5

Ephesians 3:21   I Timothy 3:15

8

THE CHURCH ON THE
MOON OR ON THE MOVE

*Therefore we also, since we are surrounded by
so great a cloud of witnesses, let us lay aside
every weight, and the sin which so easily
ensnares us, and let us run with endurance
the race that is set before us. . . . "*

HEBREWS 12:1, NKJV

WHY IS IT "BUSINESS AS USUAL" in the Church
while Rome burns? One would think the Church was on
the moon, not on the move. Many years ago I had dinner
with Richard Wurmbrand, a Romanian Christian minister
of Jewish descent. He had been arrested, imprisoned and
tortured by the communists for his beliefs. The Soviets
wished to make him an example in order to break the back
of the Church in Romania. The object was to cause him
to deny his faith. No matter how much he was tortured

or how severe the torment, they were unsuccessful, and over the course of Wormrand's persecution, he led one of his key torturers to Christ.

Wurmbrand related a story he had heard of the 1493 battle for Constantinople. The city, the capital of the Byzantine Empire, was attacked by the Ottomans under the leadership of 21-year-old Sultan Mehmed II. The Turk and his armies laid a fifty-three day siege on Constantinople. The end result of the action was the fall of the mighty Roman Empire, no small feat. It also delivered a mammoth blow to the Christian world. The Ottoman Turks were Muslim, and their victory over the Byzantines allowed them to march unrestrained into Europe without having to fear an attack on their flank.

Wurmbrand said when approached by the Christian people of Constantinople for direction on whether to fight or stand down, members of the local church council said they had no idea. They had been too busy discussing pressing matters such as: What color were the eyes of the Virgin Mary? If a fly falls into holy water, was the water defiled, or was the fly sanctified? And, what gender are angels?

When America is at war with radical Islam, and when war has also been declared on families and on the very fabric of our nation, it is time for the Church to rise up with moral clarity. Instead, much of the Church is just as distracted as the Church in Romania was in Wurmbrand's day.

God planned Pentecost before the foundation of the world was laid. The initiation of it was certainly more significant than a presidential inauguration. The strategic battle plan of Pentecost was designed to transform the world, and it did. On that day, 3,000 received the Word and were baptized. The Bible tells us, "The apostles testified powerfully to the resurrection of the Lord Jesus, and God's great blessing was upon them all." (Acts 4:33, LB)

The latter rain outpouring of God's Spirit carries the same significance as the original. (see Joel 2:23; Hosea 6:3; Zechariah 10:1 and James 5:7) Multitudes will call upon the Name of the Lord and be gloriously saved. (see Joel 2:32; Acts 2:21, 3:19 and Romans 10:13)

The Old Testament prophet Zechariah advised, "Ask ye of the LORD rain in the time of the latter rain" (Zechariah 10:1, NIV). Hosea 10:12, NIV, states: "It is time to seek the Lord until He come and rain righteousness upon us."

In preparation for Christ's imminent birth and ministry, God planned that the World would have interconnecting, straight Roman roads and a rebuilt temple. Today, He is planning for Christ's return by preparing for Himself "a glorious church without spot or wrinkle" (Ephesians 5:27, NIV), filled with powerful Believers who manifest Christ's ministry on earth. The sooner we admit to our spots and wrinkles, the quicker we can fuse with Who He is. Your perspective of Christ and His Kingdom determines the possibilities you pursue.

Hosea 6:1-2 says:

> Come, and let us return to the Lord; For He has torn, but He will heal us; He has stricken, but He will bind us up. After two days He will revive us; On the third day He will raise us up, That we may live in His sight.

Hosea said that on the third day would come the latter rain—the last great revival before Christ's return (Hosea 6:3); an unprecedented outpouring of the Holy Spirit and the final move of Christ's Spirit on this globe, greater than any the world has ever seen.

God is preparing us for His greatest move in history, which will usher in the Lord's return. Our churches will be packed on Sundays and Believers will tithe and intercede as never before. We will no longer be content with a lifestyle outside of the miraculous, but will live an overcoming, victorious life in the realm of the Holy Spirit.

When Jesus begins to march, it is time for the Church to move! God's last great awakening will plunder the hell-bound to populate heaven. Peter prophesied that there would be a mighty revival, *times of refreshing,* that would come "from the presence of the Lord." (see Acts 3:19, NIV) We are going to be changed from glory to glory. The spotlight of heaven will shine on hungry hearts, and those who thirst for righteousness will be filled.

Ordinary Believers will so fully surrender to the life of Jesus in them, that He will reveal Himself in all His glory. All His prayers that have not been answered will be answered and manifested through us. We are about to see more than mere revival and much more than an occasional move of God's Spirit.

A Christian content with status-quo and business-as-usual comfort zones, living only for Self and bound by religious pride, will be cast aside when the Father chooses His workers for the end-time harvest. Those who are content to live without Christ on the throne of their lives will miss the greatest, heavenly power-surge ever seen, empowering Believers to reap the final harvest.

Who is on the throne of your life? Many Believers would automatically reply, "God." But is that really true? Men of integrity and honor, who dare to speak out against sin, too often become targets for egotistical men who place themselves above the will and call of God. In his book *The Kingdom of Self,* Earl Jabay, a clinically trained chaplain, wrote:

> The Kingdom of Self, understand, is in our heads. We spend years building this fantasy kingdom unto our own glory. The king's thinking becomes grandiose and his feelings ultimate. He believes all things can and must be done according to his will. And another thing; the king is never wrong. He is always right. Just ask him. He'll tell you.[44]

Is your heart a place devoted only to God, or has He been crowded out by worldly endeavors and enticements? Too often we begin our walk with Him filled with good intentions; we petition God wholeheartedly to occupy first place in our lives, but eventually the world begins to intrude. Our focus shifts to jobs, friends, or our family. These are all essential parts of life, but just remember that Jesus said, "But seek first the kingdom of God and His righteousness, and all these things shall be added to you." (See Matthew 6:33, NKJV) If your priorities are in order, your motivation will be about pleasing God, putting Him first and foremost in your life, and then He will add His blessings.

We can't limit Jesus to our timetable; we have to get on His. God is not going to consult with us to determine His plan or purpose in our lives. It's our responsibility to determine if *we* are in *His* will. We have not taken over the world, because we have not been with Jesus. God has drawn the battle line, and is sending angels on assignments to gather saints who are hungry and thirsty for Jesus.

This unparalleled harvest will begin with a hunger to do the works of Christ. Believers, who are tired of faking it and tired of making excuses for not fulfilling Christ's own prophecies, will commit themselves to prayer and intimacy with Jesus. They will clearly see the person and power of the Holy Spirit, and will comprehend Christ's mission both in, and through them.

In general, today's Christians have no such sense of destiny. But if we discover Christ within us, the hope of glory, we will be more excited about the Christian life than anything the world has to offer. (See Colossians 1:27, KJV) Such enthusiasm kills inferiority, destroys the paralysis of the past and gives a brilliant view of eternity. When Christ resides in His rightful dwelling place on earth, the heavens will open for the one in whom He dwells.

On a trip to India, my daughter wept because of seeing a leper with no arms or legs. I asked a doctor about leprosy. He explained that most lepers don't lose their fingers and toes due to injury, because they're desensitized to pain, but they can inadvertently rub them off. He said in previous years, the biggest problem was the rats chewing and eating fingers and toes when the lepers went to sleep. A doctor found a cure. It was a "kitty cat." He tied a string around the leper and the other end of the string to the cat. When the rats came, the cat got the rats!

We have, leading the way for us, the Lion of the Tribe of Judah to consume the Enemy of our souls. He is in full battle gear and demons are trembling. He is clothed with the robe of righteousness and His eyes are as a flame of fire. He upholds all things by the word of His power (see Hebrews 1:3).

When we become convinced that *this* Christ dwells within in us, we will be a power that causes the enemies of the cross to quake and cower. When we're gripped with a sense of the destiny of Christ's mission and His present-day ministry, we will want to see it being operational in our lives. Who on earth has a greater sense of destiny or a greater plan than the Lord Jesus Christ? When we allow the "Lamb of God who takes away the sins of the world" to function through us, it will completely change our outlook.

Every Believer is faced with an eternal countdown clock that cannot be halted; the choice must be made whether to live in Christ or die. There is no middle ground. Not to choose life will result in death by default. To choose life is to seek after Christ with such zeal that little else matters. By inviting Christ to live in and through us, we allow the power of Christ to fulfill His present-day ministry here on earth.

God-mockers have come out of the closet; pornographers and dope sellers have crawled out of the sewer. *Now* is the time for God's blood-washed, Spirit-filled children to emerge from hiding and exalt Jesus as *the* King of Kings and Lord of Lords. God wants to see the life of His Son reproduced in our lives, to bring cataclysmic events into play through Spirit-to-spirit contact enabling Jesus to return to earth.

All of heaven will move as the power reserved for

the Son of God shines, blinding the powers of darkness. Armies will be subdued; enemies of God will flee. The work of God, the final mission of the King of glory, will be evidenced by all.

We have, for too long, been served a Christianity sandwiched between sensuality and selfishness (see Galatians 5:7). When we have been with Jesus, the Self-life will not even enter the picture. That man or woman will reap more fruit in one day than in a lifetime of attempting to live the Christian life with Self on the throne. Only the Person of the Holy Spirit can make this possible. The fullness of Christ will be manifested through us when we are truly a people who has been with Jesus, like the saints of old.

David, in a spiritual awakening, danced into Jerusalem with the Ark of the Covenant. (See 2 Samuel 6:12-23) Elijah on Mt. Carmel challenged the prophets of Baal in a nationwide awakening. (See 1 Kings 18:1-46) John the Baptist declared, "Prepare ye the way of the Lord" and, "He will baptize you with the Holy Spirit and with fire." (See Matthew 3:1-12, NIV)

The Bible says of the last days, "In that day will I raise up the tabernacle of David that is fallen." (Amos 9:11, NIV)

Indeed, the tabernacle of David has fallen. But in far more than a physical sense. King David had died. God wasn't speaking of King David; He was speaking of Christ, the *Ben David*, the son of David.

I am convinced that the temple, which the Bible says must be rebuilt before Christ's Second Coming, is a dwelling place for Christ, and *not* just a physical building. The tabernacle of David has to do with you and me! Our bodies are the dwelling place for the Spirit of Christ. God is waiting for His children to take His Word literally and become the dwelling place, the tabernacle, the temple for His Son in the most literal sense.

Peter commanded at Pentecost,

> Repent ye therefore, and be converted, that your sins may be blotted out, when the times of refreshing shall come from the presence of the Lord; and he shall send Jesus Christ, which before was preached unto you. (Acts 3:19-20, NIV)

The times of refreshing *are* coming, and Jesus Himself will reside within our tabernacle!

> ARISE [. . . to a new life]! Shine (be radiant with the glory of the Lord); for your light is come,

and the glory of the Lord is risen upon you! For behold, darkness shall cover the earth, and dense darkness [all] peoples; but the Lord shall arise upon you. . . . And nations shall come to your light, and kings to the brightness of your rising. (Isaiah 60:1-3 AMP, emphasis added)

The Lord appeared in an astounding vision to Isaiah and he saw the *kabod*, Christ's magnificent glory (Isaiah 6:1-4). The angels cried "Holy, holy, holy" as Isaiah saw the Lord sitting high and lifted up on His throne. The doorposts were moving, God's train was filling the temple and smoke was pouring out. Overwhelmed, Isaiah cried out:

Woe is me! For I am undone and ruined, because I am a man of unclean lips, and dwell in the midst of a people of unclean lips; for my eyes have seen the King, the Lord of hosts! (Isaiah 6:5, AMP)

We, like Isaiah, are unclean people in an unclean world, yet the glory of the Lord is ready to rise upon us, and nations will come to our light.

Many refuse to allow Christ to enter. We too often stand at the door of our lives saying, "Jesus, you can come into the living room, but don't touch anything." We keep

Jesus out of the bedroom, out of the television room, out of our refrigerators and certainly out of the kids' rooms. He is standing at the door ready to furnish the house with every good and pleasant thing, and we're running around tidying just enough of the house to allow Him to see a tiny part of it.

What are we denying Him access to when it's His dwelling-place? It's like saying to the person who owns the house, "You can't come in. We can meet on the front porch, but I don't want you inside because you'll gather too much information, and gain access to the private parts of my life."

Where is Christ's dwelling place going to be? We might say, "I wish someone would build that temple over there in the Middle East somewhere so the Lord can come back." Or we can say, "Here You are, Lord, You can come in and do whatever You want. I'll surrender my own thoughts about what You should do and I'll do whatever You do, with You. I won't hinder You!"

The greatest manifestation of God's glory, power and presence will come through the kind of intimacy with Jesus that provides a place in which He can dwell. Just as your soul has your body for its dwelling place, so Christ, by His Holy Spirit, wants all of you—your whole body and soul as His dwelling place to control completely. When flesh sits on the throne of your life, chaos is the norm; and the worst kind of flesh is religious flesh.

PRAYER FOR AMERICA:

Father,

I pray that America would submit totally to Your authority. Your Word tells me that I am equipped to bind Satan and take godly authority over his wiles and plans. In Mark 16:17, You said, "In My name they will cast out demons." The Enemy is stealthily trying to enter my country, America, and plunder it. I therefore, bind the evil one and cast him out in the Name of Jesus Christ. Help every American to make it a priority to gather with those of "like precious faith" and seek You, the Giver of life, light and grace. Give every Believer the strength to commit to prayer and fasting; to lift You up in songs of praise. I submit myself, to yield my life so that I can draw closer to You and be an effective prayer warrior for my beloved country. Thank You for the promises that are mine through the Word, and for the weapons of my warfare that give me the tools to resist Satan. God bless America!

SCRIPTURES FOR STUDY:

Mark 16:17	Matthew 17:19, 21
II Corinthians 6:14	James 4:7
Ephesians 4:27	Ephesians 6:11-12
Matthew 12:29	John 10:10
II Corinthians 10:4-5	Luke 10:17

9

GOD BLESS AMERICA!

Help us to recognize your voice,
help us not to be allured by the madness
of the world, so that we may never fall
away from you, O Lord Jesus Christ.

ALBRECHT DURER,
RENAISSANCE ARTIST[45]

And a stranger will they not follow,
but will flee from him: for they know
not the voice of strangers.

JOHN 10:5, KJV

WHAT WILL BE REQUIRED for God to bless America before our Lord returns? Jesus said: "Some of you won't taste death until you see My kingdom come." (Mark 9:1, NIV) What did He mean? Everyone who heard Him say that died physically. But many of them *did* see His kingdom come. They experienced the fullness of His present-day ministry. Peter saw Christ's kingdom come, and people were healed just by his shadow falling on them. Paul saw Christ's kingdom come, and people were healed when pieces of his clothing were placed on them. John saw Christ's kingdom come in the midst of a prison island, surrounded by the worst elements of society, when he was caught up in a vision of the end-times seeing Jesus in all His royal, heavenly power. These "God wrestlers" saw Christ's kingdom come in all its glory. They saw Christ's ministry fulfilled on this earth. This is the kind of power needed for the Church to throw down the gauntlet in the face of the Enemy who has come to steal our country, kill its citizens, and destroy the lives of God's people.

Western culture has softened us, causing us to settle for a comfortable what's-in-it-for-me style of Christianity, rather than sacrificing in order to have God's power and presence. I was once in the office of a presidential candidate who had publicly proclaimed his faith in Christ. I asked him what his political stance would be on what were once considered the hot issues in Christianity, like abortion.

"The way you win elections is to avoid those black-and-white issues," he responded. "Abortion is really a non-issue."

"But why?" I asked in consternation.

He replied, "Because our polls show that as many Christians have abortions as non-Christians. In fact, there is little difference in the polls between people in the Church and those outside it."

How sad. The Church doesn't vote its conscience because its conscience is guilty! So politicians stay neutral and morality is nullified.

Twenty-eight civilizations have risen and fallen. Ministries and visions have come and gone. No matter how powerful each was, they are now no more! Will that be the fate of our nation, our generation? Let's get onboard with what God is doing, so that we are not left behind. If we as Believers do what we've done in this decade, then we'll have what we had in the last decade—very little.

We must pray for Christ's mission to be accomplished. Joshua said: "Consecrate yourselves today to the Lord, and tomorrow God will do amazing things among you." (Exodus 32:29, NIV) We need a pure understanding of what it means to have Christ in us, and the effectiveness of prayer to complete His mission.

The highly respected theologian, Dr. Francis Schaeffer, penned a sobering book just before his death. In *The Great*

Evangelical Disaster, Schaeffer issued a somber and concise overview of the twentieth-century church. He wrote:

> Here is the great evangelical disaster—the failure of the evangelical world to stand up for truth as truth .... the evangelical church has accommodated to the world spirit of the age .... to accommodate to the world spirit...is nothing less than the most gross form of worldliness, we must say ... with exceptions, the evangelical church is worldly and not faithful to the living Christ.[46]

What a tragic indictment, yet how true.

If we are truly the salt and the light of the earth, why have the worldly taken over the Church? Have you been vaccinated with a mild case of Christianity so as to protect you from the real disease? Those who have tried salvation without dying to the flesh will soon fall away. In Matthew 13:3b-7, NIV, Jesus related the parable of the sower:

> A farmer went out to sow his seed. As he was scattering the seed, some fell along the path, and the birds came and ate it up. Some fell on rocky places, where it did not have much soil. It sprang up quickly, because the soil was shallow.

> But when the sun came up, the plants were
> scorched, and they withered because they had
> no root. Other seed fell among thorns, which
> grew up and choked the plants.

When given another opportunity to commit to Christ, the "seed" might say, "I tried that," as if Christ is a method to quit smoking, a medical treatment or a trendy diet.

We preach the cross, but for Christ's present-day ministry to operate in our lives and for Him to bless our nation, we must camp out at Calvary. We must invite the convicting power of the Holy Spirit into our lives, and become God's house of prayer. God wants to do today what He did two thousand years ago. He has a final blow to execute. The first great battle was at Calvary; the last great battle is at the end-of-the-age for the final harvest. This is the final assault and the finished work of the cross. This last strategic strike will render the demons of hell bound in chains, and bring in the greatest harvest of souls the world has ever known.

Christ is longing for us today to be intimate with Him. Only then can He become fully functional and fully released in us. Only then can He manifest His power, passion, and purity in order to fulfill His purpose and mission on earth through us. Only then dare we stand toe-to-toe with the Enemy and shout, "Satan, you can't have my country! You can't have America!"

You and I are to become "the measure of the stature of the fullness of Christ," but that is only possible when Christ is fully functional in us. (See Ephesians 4:13, AMP)

In Isaiah 6, the prophet laid face-down in the Temple. He was exhausted from interceding for the children of Israel, and as his supplications filled the Temple, Jehovah responded with a vision for the prophet's eyes only. Isaiah was transported from the earthly Temple into the very throne room of God. There, his attention was not captured by the beauty of his surroundings, but was centered on the One whose Presence was overwhelming. God was reassuring Isaiah that He, Judah's Supreme King, was on the throne for all time and eternity. Isaiah described God's appearance:

> In the year that King Uzziah died, I saw the Lord, high and exalted, seated on a throne; and the train of his robe filled the temple. Above him were seraphim, each with six wings: With two wings they covered their faces, with two they

covered their feet, and with two they were flying. And they were calling to one another: "Holy, holy, holy is the Lord Almighty; the whole earth is full of His glory." At the sound of their voices the doorposts and thresholds shook and the temple was filled with smoke. (Isaiah 6:1–4, NIV)

No matter who sits on the thrones of earthly leadership, whether king, president, or prime minister, God is ultimately in control. No one ascends to office or holds it without God having allowed them to be placed there. Psalm 75:6–7, NIV, tells us:

For exaltation comes neither from the east nor from the west nor from the south. But God is the Judge: He puts down one, and exalts another.

Daniel reminds us in chapter 2:20–21, NIV:

Blessed be the name of God forever and ever, for wisdom and might are His. And He changes the times and the seasons; He removes kings and raises up kings; He gives wisdom to the wise and knowledge to those who have understanding.

And Solomon wrote in Proverbs 21:1, NIV:

The king's heart is in the hand of the Lord,
like the rivers of water; He turns it wherever
He wishes.

Isaiah's vision reminds me a little of standing before a magistrate in a courtroom. Dressed in black robes, he or she sits elevated above the others in the court. The judge is in charge, and holds the gavel that can dispatch anyone with a single motion. Like Isaiah, we stand in awe of earthly authority; how much more should we stand in awe of the God of the universe!

Why do most churches have small crowds at every service, other than Sunday morning? Why do only 20 percent of Christians tithe regularly? Why do we have to train and urge Christians to witness to others, instead of having a compassionate life force that naturally flows from within us? Why is the prayer ministry at most churches generally the least attended of all services?

As the Church, we sit in pews week-after-week, unchanged because we do not have a vision of our true destiny in Christ. We don't understand what the life of Christ within us can accomplish, so we fall back confidently on our fleshly works and are powerless against the Enemy of God. We must gain a profound sense of the mission of Christ Who dwells within us. Christ will fulfill His ministry by delegating to us. The Pharisees in Jesus' time didn't get it; the religious Pharisees today *still* don't get it.

There is a world of difference between being religious, and having a personal encounter with Christ; the difference we're talking about today. There is a world of difference between trying to live the Christian life, and having Christ live His life *through* us. Religion gives us existence; Jesus gives us life. The flesh gives us today; Jesus gives us eternity.

God has promised He would move Heaven and earth for those in hot pursuit of Him. He did just that at Calvary. A blast of evil is shaking the earth so strongly today, that even sincere Christians, who are trying to live the Christian life, *without* surrendering control, will be devastated by its darkness. They will find themselves in their own sheltered bunkers, facing a roaring cry of human agony with no power. It's time for the mouth of hell to experience the steel punch of people who have been with Jesus. In spite of the doctrines of devils and the philosophies of fools, scoffing at the cross and the blood, the Lord of Glory will have the final word on this planet.

Only one thing will allow Satan to disqualify us from being part of the greatest movement of God in history, and that is the refusal to dethrone Self. Once we die to Self, we will make a God-connection. The natural will come in contact with the supernatural and hell will be shaken. Worry will be a thing of the past because we then will see our problems from our position in Christ. We will be ruling and reigning with Him in the now.

Second only to God's magnificence as seen by Isaiah in chapter 6 is His holiness—His unparalleled purity. Even as the prophet was mesmerized by the presence of God, he could hear a sound that he identified as a chorus of angelic beings:

> And one cried to another and said: "Holy, holy, holy is the Lord of hosts; the whole earth is full of His glory!" And the posts of the door were shaken by the voice of him who cried out, and the house was filled with smoke. (Isaiah 6:3, NIV)

Isaiah had entered into the presence of God and would come away with a renewed conviction of the holiness of God. It cannot be trivialized or marginalized. God is holy! He is so much more superior and resplendent than anything man can imagine. No earthly king can match His grandeur or His majesty. His very presence demands worship, devotion, and wonder.

God is love! God is holy! God is righteous! That doesn't mean that God meets the standard for those qualities; God *is* the standard by which all else is measured. Isaiah had entered into the presence of the epitome of holiness—Jehovah God. It is the character of the great I AM! As we saw earlier, Isaiah's response in verse 5 was immediate:

> Woe is me, for I am undone! Because I am a man of unclean lips, and I dwell in the midst of a people of unclean lips; for my eyes have seen the King, the Lord of hosts.

At the time of Isaiah's vision, Israel was at a crossroads—the people were economically prosperous but spiritually bankrupt. As one writer noted, Isaiah dwelled in the midst of "fat and happy sinners."[47]

The prophet, in the presence of pure holiness, realized his unworthiness. He had been concerned with the sinfulness of Judah; now he was concerned with his own impurity when seen under the microscope of God's purity. Isaiah realized he had no place to hide—he was doomed.

As he lay prostrate before the Lord God Almighty, he cried that he was a man of unclean lips and he dwelled in the midst of a people whose lips were unclean. Jehovah, however, did not abandon Isaiah to his woeful status, for He is the God of redemption:

> Then one of the seraphim flew to me with a live coal in his hand, which he had taken with tongs from the altar. With it he touched my mouth and said, "See, this has touched your lips; your guilt is taken away and your sin atoned for." (Isaiah 6:6–7, NIV)

What is our reaction when we realize the holiness of God? Do we truly grasp its meaning? Do we dishonor God to the point that He simply becomes our pal rather than the holy and righteous God? A true encounter with God always brings inevitable change. Either your commitment to Him grows deeper, or you harden your heart and perish spiritually. Psalm 93:2 reminds us that God's throne is everlasting—it always has been and forever will be.

In Lamentations 5:19, Jeremiah cried, "You, O Lord, remain forever; Your throne from generation to generation." What better assurance could we have than to know that God is on His throne and beside Him sits the "Lamb slain from the foundation of the world." (See Revelation 13:8) It is a position of absolute power and command. Nothing surprises God; He knows before a thought makes its way into our consciousness what we are going to do. He knows the answer even before we know the question. He is aware of the solution even before we encounter the problem. Because He occupies the throne on high and can see the end from the beginning. According to theologian Arthur W. Pink:

> Divine sovereignty means that God is God in fact, as well as in name, that He is on the Throne of the universe, directing all things, working all things "after the counsel of His own will" (Eph. 1:11).[48]

Daily events portend change, yet God never changes. He is faithful and immovable. Songsmith Dottie Rambo wrote the spiritual "I Go to the Rock." The chorus reminds us:

> The earth all around me is sinking sand
> But on Jesus the solid Rock I stand
> When I need a shelter
> When I need a friend
> I go to the Rock[49]

Perhaps the writer of Hebrews said it best and most succinctly in chapter 13, verse 8: "Jesus Christ is the same yesterday, today, and forever."

Have you heard the old saying, "When the going gets tough; the tough get going"? The reality is: "When the going gets tough, go to Jesus!" It is a move you will never regret; for it is there that you will find the help you need. It is in His presence that you will find the strength to battle the Enemy.

Hebrews 4:16 reminds us that as Believers, because of our relationship with Christ, we can "come boldly to the throne of grace, that we may obtain mercy and find grace to help in time of need."

There are those who place great value in who they know—especially if those persons are considered to be the movers and shakers of the world. Those "in the know" will quickly recite a litany of who's who and what's what in order to impress others. But you and I are intimately acquainted with the only One who really matters—God the Father. We are heirs of God and joint heirs with Jesus Christ, and are sealed by the Holy Spirit. (See Ephesians 1:13–14) Because we have a close, personal relationship with the triune Godhead, we have the privilege of entering the throne room anytime we choose. Revelation 5:8 says that the prayers of the saints are "golden bowls full of incense."

Unlike those who may spend great sums of money to hobnob with the "A-listers," our entrée is a gift freely given, and yet it cost Jesus everything. God's grace has made it possible for us to have continual access to the throne and He who sits upon it.

In 1 John 5:14–15, the apostle wrote these words of encouragement to the followers of Christ:

> Now this is the confidence that we have in Him, that if we ask anything according to His will, He hears us. And if we know that He hears us, whatever we ask, we know that we have the petitions that we have asked of Him.

As obedient children, we know we can approach His throne with the assurance that if we ask according to His will, Jehovah will hear and respond. That, my friend, is the most important relationship you and I can have. Prostrating ourselves at the foot of the cross in prayer and supplication will move God to bless America again!

PRAYER FOR AMERICA:

I pray, Lord God of heaven,

O great and awesome God, *You* who keep *Your* covenant and mercy with those who love You and observe Your commandments, please let Your ear be attentive and Your eyes open, that You may hear the prayer of Your servant which I pray before You now, day and night, for the children of Israel Your servants, and confess the sins of the children of Israel which we have sinned against You. Both my father's house and I have sinned. We have acted very corruptly against You, and have not kept the commandments, the statutes, nor the ordinances which You commanded of Your servant Moses. Remember, I pray, the word that You commanded Your servant Moses, saying, '*If* you are unfaithful, I will scatter you among the nations; but *if* you return to Me, and keep My commandments and do them, though some of you were cast out to the farthest part of the heavens, *yet* I will gather them from there, and bring them to the place which I have chosen as a dwelling for My name.' Now these *are* Your servants and Your people, whom You have redeemed by Your great power, and by Your strong hand. O Lord, I pray, please let Your ear be attentive to the prayer of Your servant, and to the prayer of Your servants who desire to fear Your name. . .

SCRIPTURES FOR STUDY:

Psalm 34:17   Psalm 107:6

Psalm 40:17   Psalm 50:15

Psalm 34:4   Galatians 5:1

John 8:32   Romans 6:7-19

II Peter 2:9

10

THE KEY TO SPIRITUAL WARFARE

Now they saw the boldness of Peter and John, and
perceived that they were unlearned and ignorant
men, they marveled; and they took knowledge
of them, that they had been with Jesus.

ACTS 4:13

ETCHED INTO THE WALL in the lobby of the original CIA headquarters building in Washington, DC to characterize the intelligence mission of a free society are these words: "And ye shall know the Truth and the Truth shall make you free," (John 8:32, KJV.) Those words are prophetic and must be the banner for every God-fearing American today.

The question must now be asked: How do we successfully conduct spiritual warfare in order to know the truth and save our country, America? The answer: Success will only come when we plug ourselves fully into the source of all answered prayer. Nothing can replace time spent in prayer and intercession in the presence of Jesus.

Why is this so important? One of the signers of the Declaration of Independence, Samuel Huntington, warned the colonists:

> While the great body of freeholders are acquainted with the duties which they owe to their God, to themselves, and to men, they will remain free. But if ignorance and depravity should prevail, they will inevitably lead to slavery and ruin.[50]

The Revolutionary War was fought by men—and yes, women—who gave their lives to live in freedom in the United States of America. The apostle Paul warned of returning to that from which we have been made free: "For freedom Christ has set us free; stand firm therefore, and do not submit again to a yoke of slavery." (Galatians 5:1, ESV)

In Acts, chapter 9, Paul (then Saul) truly met the God of the impossible—the One who was born a baby, lived as a man, suffered death on the cross, rose again the third day, and now sits at the right hand of God making intercession for His beloved children. Saul was miraculously changed, including his name. In verse 16 of that chapter, God reveals that He will show Paul the things he must suffer for the Gospel, and still the apostle was willing to step out in faith and follow in the footsteps of Jesus. Paul had to face the seemingly impossible assignment of leaving behind his old life of "breathing threats and murder against the disciples of the Lord" (see Acts 9:1) and preach the message of Christ.

You may think it an impossible task to turn America from its present course back to faith in God. The impossible often begins with one small step. When God created Adam, He began with a handful of dust. Moses was sent to challenge Pharaoh with a walking stick; Samson killed thousands of Philistines with the jawbone of a donkey (see Judges 15); Jesus fed the multitudes with a couple of fish and five loaves of bread. Small beginnings, to be sure! When God sent David to conquer a giant, the shepherd didn't take a cannon; he picked up small stones. When God sent His son to earth, He wasn't sent to a metropolis, but to the small, backwater hamlet of Bethlehem. In Zechariah 4:10 (NLT), the prophet says, "Do not despise these small beginnings, for the LORD rejoices to see the work begin." Do you think your ideas are too small to succeed? Give them to God and let Him anoint you for the impossible.

Have *you* been with Jesus? Spending time with Him is the only way to prepare for spiritual warfare. God wants us to live and breathe in Him. Jesus will be manifested in the lives of praying saints in order to gather in the final harvest. They will form the army described in the book of Joel; one that will witness the end-time ministry of Jesus on this earth.

Have you been with *Jesus*? It is in Him that we "live and move and have our being." (See Acts 17:28) We need to walk with Jesus on such a consistent basis that His voice is always clear to us, and we are ever ready to perform His will.

Can those around you tell that you have been with Jesus? The eighth prayer of Jesus in John 17 was that people would know God had sent Him and that they would also know we, His followers, are just as loved by God as He was. (See John 17:22-23, 25 and Acts 4:13) How can the world know how much God loves us unless His love becomes outwardly evident in our lives? Successful spiritual warfare demands that we spend time with the

Author and Finisher of our faith. (See Hebrews 12:2) Jesus told His disciples what was necessary to walk with Him:

> If any of you wants to be my follower ... you must put aside your selfish ambition, shoulder your cross, and follow me. If you try to keep your life for yourself, you will lose it. But if you give up your life for my sake and for the sake of the Good News, you will find true life. (Mark 8:34-35 NLT)

Truthfully, when only one person dares to spend time with Jesus in prayer and the practice of spiritual warfare, it can change an entire generation. William Seymour, an indigent, one-eyed, discouraged African American living in the time before the civil rights movement, was such a man. This touch on his life inspired him to spend time with Jesus. This heretofore unknown man began holding meetings in a burned-out mission building on Azusa Street in Los Angeles. From this came a revival that has proven to be one of the greatest strategic victories in Christian history.

Status quo Christianity doesn't work when engaged in spiritual warfare; Christ-centered Christianity does. We need a vibrant relationship with a living God that will allow His power to change our lives and the lives of those around us. God desires to do great things through us, if we are only willing to be with Him and walk where He directs us. Spending time with Jesus is not something we do once; it is something we live breath by breath.

Turning America back to God will require commitment. Christian political activist and author David Barton and researcher George Barna wrote:

> Keep in mind: No nation that has resisted doing it God's way has ever prevailed. Objectively speaking, there is no reason to believe that ours will be the first. . . . Do not get caught up in the focus of what "the nation" must do. Every one of us must slow down, take time to examine ourselves, and figure out what commitments we personally must make to pull our weight in the national turnaround.
>
> It is so much easier to point a finger at society and wait for it to change. But that's not how cultural transformation works. It takes place one life at a time, and the first life that must change is yours.[51]

Prayer is the most powerful weapon in Heaven's arsenal, and brings with it the promise of the blessings of God. Just ask Esther if prayer changes things! She came to the king in fear for her life but left with supernatural favor. She came with poverty but left with prosperity. She came in despair but departed highly favored. She came representing a people who were marked for destruction and left the king's presence with a way of escape for her people.

Daniel engaged in intercession in chapter 10 and changed nations. For twenty-one days, the prophet had immersed himself in prayer. As he sought the face of God, an angel appeared. The angel had startling news for him and for those of us who have prayed earnestly and diligently. The "prince of Persia," apparently one of Lucifer's fallen angels, had hindered the answer to Daniel's prayer. Why is it important to know this? Persistence in prayer pays dividends! Had Daniel not continued to intercede until the battle in the heavenlies was won, his prayers would have gone unanswered.

King Hezekiah was faced with the threat of annihilation. The king of Assyria made the unfortunate mistake of thinking that Hezekiah trusted only in horses, chariots, and his alliance with Egypt. Using the "town crier" method of communication, the commander-in-chief of the Assyrian army stood in the midst of the town square and taunted Hezekiah. He proclaimed that *Yahweh* himself had sent the Assyrians to defeat Judah.

When the king's threats were delivered to Hezekiah in the form of a written dispatch, he did the one most important thing he could have done. . . he went to the temple, spread the letter on the altar, and prostrated himself before God. Hezekiah prayed:

> Now therefore, O Lord our God, I pray, save us from his hand, that all the kingdoms of the earth may know that You are the Lord God, You alone. (II Kings 19:19, NKJV)

God spoke the answer to Hezekiah's prayer through the prophet Isaiah: "For I will defend this city, to save it For My own sake and for My servant David's sake." (Isaiah 37:35, NKJV) The king could have heard no sweeter words than the promise that God would defend his nation.

After David was anointed by Samuel, there came a morning when his father, Jesse, ordered his youngest son to take supplies to David's brothers who were battling the Philistines in the Valley of Elah. Upon his arrival, David saw the imposing figure of Goliath and heard the challenge being hurled across the valley to his quaking audience on the other side. David was incensed that no one in Saul's army had the courage to face the giant. They all stood on the sidelines, intimidated by the ferocity of the huge warrior. But David was not foolhardy; he knew beyond a doubt that only through the power of God could anyone defeat this adversary. He asked those around him what would be the reward for the one who slayed the enemy. David's brothers were angered by his question and began to ridicule him. He then marched before Saul and offered to fight the giant.

When Saul questioned both his youth and ability, David replied:

> I have been taking care of my father's sheep and goats. . . . When a lion or a bear comes to steal a lamb from the flock, I go after it with a club and rescue the lamb from its mouth. If the animal turns on me, I catch it by the jaw and club it to death. I have done this to both lions and bears, and I'll do it to this pagan Philistine, too, for he has defied the armies of the living God! The Lord who rescued me from the claws

of the lion and the bear will rescue me from this
Philistine! (I Samuel 17:34–37, NLT)

David was a man of great humility; he knew that he
was unable to do anything except through the power of
God. He declined to accept any commendation for his feats;
he gave God sole credit. He boldly assured Saul that God
would stand with the man who dared go forth in His name;
that God would give him the victory. In humility, David
submitted himself as an instrument in his Father's hands.

King Saul offered David his personal armor for the
battle with Goliath. After having tried it on, the young
man realized that the covering made by mortal hands
was insufficient for the task. Like the apostle Paul, David
understood he was only safe when covered with the full
armor of God. He would be vulnerable in Saul's armor;
but he would be invincible wrapped in the presence of
Jehovah-Sabaoth—the Lord our Protector.

In this modern-day "me first" society, instead of doing
it God's way, we've done it our own way, and the results
have been devastating.

David learned as a shepherd that spiritual warfare
is best undertaken when God is invited through prayer.

When he faced the giant, David was prepared. Crossing a brook, he selected five smooth stones and dropped them in his shepherd's bag. As he approached the valley, Goliath began to fling insults:

> He said to David, "Am I a dog, that you come at me with sticks?" And the Philistine cursed David by his gods. "Come here," he said, "and I'll give your flesh to the birds and the wild animals!" (I Samuel 17:43-44, NIV)

David's battle cry was simply, "I come against you in the name of the Lord Almighty, the God of the armies of Israel, whom you have defied." (I Samuel 17:45b, NIV)

Satan has flung down the gauntlet at the feet of every Believer. His threats are designed to cause you to turn and run in fear. But, God! In the end, Goliath lay on the ground—a stone embedded deeply in his forehead. David used the giant's own weapon to lop off his head and give Israel the victory—not by might, nor by power, but by the Spirit of the Lord of hosts, (Zechariah 4:6, paraphrased).

The New Testament, too, is rife with instances of prayer petitions answered and people delivered—Peter from prison, John the Revelator from death on the Isle of

Patmos, Paul from drowning at sea. Paul's ringing declaration while being tossed to and fro on the ship resonates: "For there stood by me this night an angel of the God to whom I belong and whom I serve." (Acts 27:23, NKJV)

It is never too late for God to come to the aid of His children, and prayer is the means by which we touch Him. Prayer is the key to successful spiritual warfare, and God has equipped Believers with the weapons needed to rout the Enemy. Paul instructed the Church in Ephesus in Ephesians 6:10-18a, NKJV:

> Finally, my brethren, be strong in the Lord and in the power of His might. Put on the whole armor of God, that you may be able to stand against the wiles of the devil. For we do not wrestle against flesh and blood, but against principalities, against powers, against the rulers of the darkness of this age, against spiritual *hosts* of wickedness in the heavenly *places*. Therefore take up the whole armor of God, that you may be able to withstand in the evil day, and having done all, to stand. Stand therefore, having girded your waist with truth, having put on the breastplate of righteousness, and having shod

your feet with the preparation of the gospel of peace; above all, taking the shield of faith with which you will be able to quench all the fiery darts of the wicked one. And take the helmet of salvation, and the sword of the Spirit, which is the word of God; praying always with all prayer and supplication in the Spirit.

The Church must realize, as Paul said In II Corinthians 10:3-5, NKJV:

> For though we walk in the flesh, we do not war according to the flesh. For the weapons of our warfare *are* not carnal but mighty in God for pulling down strongholds, casting down arguments and every high thing that exalts itself against the knowledge of God, bringing every thought into captivity to the obedience of Christ.

Believers in America are faced with a clear fork in the road. How will we respond? Will we take up the full armor of God and engage in the kind of spiritual warfare that touches the heart of God and turns His head? Or will we once again become members of the "silent majority", sit on the sidelines and watch this nation go up in smoke?

You and I have been equipped with everything necessary, not to run from the Enemy, but to "fight the good fight." (See I Timothy 1:18) We can say boldly, "Satan, you can't have my country, America!"

> For I, the LORD your God,
> will hold your right hand,
> Saying to you, 'Fear not, I will help you.'
> (Isaiah 41:13, NKJV)

A PRAYER:

TO EQUIP THE SAINTS FOR
SPIRITUAL WARFARE:

Father,

America needs revival and restoration. Spiritual warfare is the method; Jesus is the key. He has provided me with weapons of warfare to pull down the strongholds of the Enemy, and with the armor for protection. I have on truth, the breastplate of righteousness and on my feet I have the preparation of the Gospel of peace. I hold in one hand the shield of faith with which I can divert every fiery dart of the Enemy, and in the other I clutch the sword of the Spirit which is Your Word. You have said that no weapon formed against me shall prosper, and that the "weapons of our warfare are not carnal but mighty in God for pulling down strongholds, casting down arguments and every high thing that exalts itself against the knowledge of God." You have called me to "Submit to God. Resist the devil and he will flee from you." Therefore, I say to the Enemy, Satan, you can't have my country, for greater is He that is in me than he that is in the world!

SCRIPTURES FOR STUDY:

II Corinthians 10:4-5	James 4:7	Ephesians 6:12
II Corinthians 10:3-4	Zechariah 4:6	John 16:33
Revelation 12:10	I Corinthians 16:13	Joshua 1:9
I Peter 5:8	Ephesians 6:18	

THE SPIRIT WAR

Likewise the Spirit also helps in our weaknesses.
For we do not know what we should pray for as we
ought, but the Spirit Himself makes intercession
for us with groanings which cannot be uttered.
Now He who searches the hearts knows what the
mind of the Spirit is, because He makes intercession
for the saints according to the will of God.

ROMANS 8:26-27, NKJV

THE BATTLE FOR THE SOUL of America is a spirit battle; one between two spirits, two books and two kingdoms. Today's Goliath is not a visible enemy, but a spiritual enemy. Demons do not clear customs, and with advances in technology, neither do their earth-bound minions. Knowledge is doubling every thirteen months and with Internet developments, will soon double every twelve hours. Modern man speaks only one language; that of computers that navigate the cyber-world.

Today, the depth of a book must compete with the speed of the screen. The screen hypnotizes, but ultimately distorts. The Internet is the superhighway that radical Islam employs to recruit its followers. No one could ever have predicted at the beginning of the twentieth century that the United States would be at war which has an enemy with no borders, no conventional military, and no specific nationality. It is an enemy with no face and a name many in America refuse to speak—radical Islam. Radical Islam has to be fought just like Americans fought the Nazis during World War II. We will not change their minds; we will not win them over; we will not pacify them. The only way to defeat them is through moral clarity. There are no "good terrorists."

This battle has never been fully fought by the ones capable of winning: the Church. I am not speaking of a building that is entered only on Sunday. How can the United States of America fight a spirit war? It must be waged and won by Spirit-filled Believers prayerfully binding principalities and powers and spiritual wickedness.

The demon-inspired cult of radical Islam is united. Bible-believers must also unite! Defeating Israel is not the ultimate objective of radical Islam; nor is Paris, France.

It is America! America is hated because it is considered a Christian nation, and because of its place of power in the world.

Radical Islamists do not fear the United States of America. The signal has gone out to millions of raging fundamentalists that America is afraid of them. Every time our Commander in Chief says there will be no boots on the ground, it is interpreted as fear. As I noted in a previous chapter, but certainly worth repeating here, Ephesians 6:10-12, NKJV, declares:

> Finally, my brethren, be strong in the Lord and in the power of His might. Put on the whole armor of God, that you may be able to stand against the wiles of the devil. For we do not wrestle against flesh and blood, but against principalities, against powers, against the rulers of the darkness of this age, against spiritual *hosts* of wickedness in the heavenly *places*.

This battle can be won through moral clarity and the power or prayer. Yes, America must be willing to face radical Islam militarily, but the "heavy lifting" must be done by Americans engaged in "effective, fervent prayer." (See James 5:16)

Hebrews 11:33-34, LB, reminds us:

> These people all trusted God and as a result won
> battles, overthrew kingdoms, ruled their people
> well, and received what God had promised them;
> they were kept from harm in a den of lions and
> in a fiery furnace. Some, through their faith,
> escaped death by the sword. Some were made
> strong again after they had been weak or sick.
> Others were given great power in battle; they
> made whole armies turn and run away.

Psalm 46:1-3 also encourages the Believer:

> God is our refuge and strength, a tested help in
> times of trouble. And so we need not fear even if
> the world blows up and the mountains crumble
> into the sea. Let the oceans roar and foam; let
> the mountains tremble!

This war cannot be won if God's people sleep. A thousand
times no! September 11 was planned and won before the first
plane left the ground. America was asleep at the post while
demons were working overtime. Jews in Jerusalem were
just as shocked on March 16, 587 BC when Nebuchadnezzar
besieged their capital and they were dragged into captivity.

This is a war between light and darkness. Let me remind you again what the prophet Ezekiel said in chapter 33, verse 6, NKJV:

> But if the watchman sees the sword coming and does not blow the trumpet, and the people are not warned, and the sword comes and takes *any* person from among them, he is taken away in his iniquity; but his blood I will require at the watchman's hand.

It is reiterated in Isaiah 62:6-7, NKJV:

> I have set watchmen on your walls, O Jerusalem; They shall never hold their peace day or night. You who make mention of the LORD, do not keep silent, And give Him no rest till He establishes And till He makes Jerusalem a praise in the earth.

II Corinthians 3:17, NKJV, states:

> Now, the Lord is the Spirit; and where the Spirit of the Lord *is*, there *is* liberty.

When God's Spirit is present, there is liberty and freedom. When the Spirit is present, there is dominion. It is time for the Church of the Living God to arise. Jonathan

Stockstill wrote "Let the Church Rise." The chorus of the song reminds us:

> Let the Church rise from the ashes
> Let the Church fall to her knees
> Let us be light in the darkness
> Let the Church rise.

The Good News today is that God still moves through His Holy Spirit!

I leave you with these scriptures:

> At that time Michael shall stand up, The great prince who stands *watch* over the sons of your people; And there shall be a time of trouble, Such as never was since there was a nation, *Even* to that time. And at that time your people shall be delivered, Every one who is found written in the book. And many of those who sleep in the dust of the earth shall awake, Some to everlasting life, Some to shame *and* everlasting contempt. Those who are wise shall shine Like the brightness of the firmament, And those who turn many to righteousness Like the stars forever and ever. (Daniel 12:1-3, NKJV)

And in Isaiah 40:15, 17, 30-31, NKJV:

> Behold, the nations *are* as a drop in a bucket,
> And are counted as the small dust on the scales;
> Look, He lifts up the isles as a very little thing.…
> All nations before Him *are* as nothing, And
> they are counted by Him less than nothing and
> worthless. . . .Even the youths shall faint and
> be weary, And the young men shall utterly fall,
> But those who wait on the LORD Shall renew
> *their* strength; They shall mount up with wings
> like eagles, They shall run and not be weary,
> They shall walk and not faint.

ENDNOTES

1. https://en.wikipedia.org/wiki/Bataclan_(theatre); accessed November 2015.

2. Josh Homme and Jesse Hughes, "Who'll Kiss the Devil," http://www.metrolyrics.com/kiss-the-devil-lyrics-eagles-of-death-metal.html; accessed November 2015.

3. http://sermons.worldchallenge.org/en/node/2235; Accessed November 2015.

4. Patrick Henry, March 23, 1775, http://libertyonline.hypermall.com/henry-liberty.html; accessed November 2015.

5. http://www.ushistory.org/valleyforge/washington/earnestprayer.html; accessed November 2015.

6. http://www.singingnews.com/news/industry-news/11642182; accessed, November 2015.

7. http://www.prayingscriptures.com/nations.shtml; accessed November 2015.

8. Peter Cartwright, *Autobiography of Peter Cartwright, The Backwoods Preacher*, W. P. Strickland, ed. (New York: Carlton Porter, 1856), pp. 30–31, 34–38, 45–52; http://www.jewishencyclopedia.com/articles/767-adams-john; accessed November 2011.

9. Max Lucado, *And the Angels Were Silent* (Sisters, Oregon: Multnomah Press, 1992), pp. 56–57.

10. Barbara Kingsolver, *Milwaukee Journal Sentinel*, September 27, 2001, http://www.rightwingnews.com/quotes/left.php; accessed November 2015.

11. Thomas Jefferson, "Commerce between Master and Slave," 1782. Available online at http://douglassarchives.org/jeff_a51.htm

12. *Holy Trinity Church v. United States*. 143 U.S. 457, 465 (February 29, 1892).

13. Ibid., 471.

14. "Great Quotes on Prayer," http://powertochange.com/experience/spiritual-growth/prayerquotes/; accessed November 2015.

15.   A reference to Jeremiah 6:14.

16.   A reference to Matthew 20:6.

17.   Martin Luther King, Jr, *Strength to Love*, pt. 4, Ch. 3 (1963).

18.   http://www.islamic-awareness.org/History/Islam/Inscriptions/DoTR.html; accessed November 2015.

19.   Aaron Klein, "Top Cleric: Jews to Build New Temple for Devil Worship," *World Net Daily*, October 19, 2015, http://www.wnd.com/2015/10/top-cleric-jews-to-build-new-temple-for-devil-worship/#uSkIPWGTdPYG0bJD.99; accessed November 2015.

20.   Victoria Shannon, "Paris Attacks: What We Know and Don't Know," *New York Times*, http://www.msn.com/en-us/news/world/paris-attacks-what-we-know-and-don%e2%80%99t-know/ar-BBn06xw?li=AAa0dzB; accessed November 2015.

21.   http://www.thebeckoning.com/poetry/yeats/yeats5.html

22.   David B. Barrett and Todd M. Johnson, *World Christian Trends a.d. 30–a.d. 2200: Interpreting the Annual Christian Megacensus*. (Pasadena, CA: William Carey Library, 2001), 243-244. According to the totals of the chart on these pages, about 6 million Christians died as martyrs to their faith out of the 40 to 55 million killed during World War II.

23.   *David Gelernter, The Wall Street Journal, October 8, 2001, http://www.wsj.com/articles/SB1002494587247149400; accessed November 2015.*

24.   George Barna, "Telling the Truth," http://www.georgebarna.com/2011/10/telling-the-truth-2/; accessed November 2015.

25.   Holly Reed, "Jonathan Edwards," Boston Collaborative Encyclopedia of Modern Western Theology, 2004, http://people.bu.edu/wwildman/bce/mwt_themes_420_edwards.htm; accessed October 2012.

26.   C. D. Harriger, http://www.crrange.com/comment107.html; accessed November 2015.

27.   Cullen Murphy, *Are We Rome? The Fall of the Empire and the Fate of America* (New York, NY: First Mariner Books, 2008), 18.

28. Robert Spencer, "Vladimir Putin: Leader of the Free World?, September 12, 2013, http://www.frontpagemag.com/fpm/204092/vladimir-putin-leader-free-world-robert-spencer; accessed November 2015.

29. Lawrence Lessig, *Republic, Lost (How Money Corrupts Congress and a Plan to Stop It)* (New York, NY: Hachette Book Group, 2011), 139.

30. http://quotes.liberty-tree.ca/quote_blog/Benjamin.Franklin.Quote.21EA; accessed November 2015.

31. Dr. Richard Lee, "Seven Principles of the Judeo-Christian Ethic," http://www.sermoncentral.com/articlec.asp?article=Richard-Lee-7-Principles-Judeo-Christian-Ethic&Page=1&ac=&csplit=9060; accessed November 2015.

32. http://www.brainyquote.com/quotes/keywords/conformity.html; accessed November 2015.

33. Rev. Mr. George Whitefield, "The Great Danger of Conformity to the World," http://quintapress.macmate.me/PDF_Books/The_great_Danger_of_Conformity_to_the_World.pdf; accessed November 2015.

34. Bill Crowder, *Our Daily Bread*, 2011, http://odb.org/2011/12/28/choices-and-consequences/; accessed November 2015.

35. http://www.foundingfatherquotes.com/quote/677#.VDQ3UI10w3E; accessed October 2014.

36. http://historicwords.com/american-history/john-adams-our-constitution-was-made-only-for-a-moral-and-religious-people/; accessed October 2014.

37. Natan Sharansky, *The Case for Democracy: The Power of Freedom to Overcome Tyranny & Terror* (New York: Public Affairs, 2004), 40–41.

38. Ronald Wilson Reagan, http://www.quotationspage.com/quote/33737.html; accessed December 2006.

39. Alexander I. Solzhenitsyn, "A World Split Apart," June 8, 1978, Harvard University Graduation, http://www.orthodoxytoday.org/articles/SolzhenitsynHarvard.php; accessed October 2014.

40. Fay Voshell, "The Choice Before Us," *American Thinker*, http://www.americanthinker.com/articles/2014/11/the_choice_before_us.html, November 2, 2014; accessed November 2014.

41. C.S. Lewis quotes, http://www.goodreads.com/quotes/19968-i-live-in-the-managerial-age-in-a-world-of; accessed November 2015.

42. Ronald Reagan, "The Evil Empire: Remarks at the Annual Convention of the National Association of Evangelicals," *American Rhetoric*, March 8, 1983, http://www.americanrhetoric.com/speeches/ronaldreaganevilempire.htm; accessed November 2014..

43. http://www.allthelyrics.com/lyrics/charles_wesley/a_charge_to_keep_i_have-lyrics-1129014.html; accessed October 2014.

44. Earl Jabay, *The Kingdom of Self,* Logos International, 1980; as quoted on http://jollyblogger.typepad.com/jollyblogger/2008/07/what-if-its-jus.html; accessed August 2014.

45. http://www.brainyquote.com/quotes/keywords/lord_jesus_christ.html#ZuIGKuyZcq0HEkr6.99; accessed November 2015.

46. Dr. Francis A. Schaeffer, The Great Evangelical Disaster (Westchester, IL: Crossway Books, 1984), 37.

47. Johnold Strey, "Three Lessons About the Triune God," http://pastorstrey.wordpress.com/2009/06/08/sermon-on-isaiah-6/; accessed August 2014.

48. A. W. Pink, "The Attributes of God," http://www.pbministries.org/books/pink/Attributes/attrib_06.htm; accessed August 2014.

49. Dottie Rambo, "I Go to the Rock," http://www.southern-gospel-music-lyrics.com/dottie-rambo-i-go-to-the-rock.html; accessed August 2014.

50. http://www.thefederalistpapers.org/founders/samuel-huntington/samuel-huntington-debates-in-the-several-state-conventions-on-the-adoption-of-the-federal-constitution-january-9-1788; accessed November 2015.

51. George Barna and David Barton, *U-Turn: Restoring America to the Strength of its Roots* (Lake Mary, FL: Charisma House Book Group, 2014), 203

MICHAEL DAVID EVANS

is a #1 *New York Times* bestselling author
of more than 60 books. His articles have appeared
in newspapers worldwide, including *USA Today*,
The Jerusalem Post, *Washington Times*, and
the *Wall Street Journal*. He has appeared on
hundreds of USA television and radio shows.

Evans was the first American to predict the
occurrence of a 9-11 more than a decade before it
happened and also the first to predict the rise of ISIS,
radical Islam's new caliphate in his 2007 #1 *New York
Times'* bestseller *The Final Move Beyond Iraq*.

Evans is the founder of the Jerusalem Prayer Team,
the Ten Boom Holocaust Center in Haarlem, Holland
and the Friends of Zion Museum in Jerusalem.

BOOKS BY: MIKE EVANS

Israel: America's Key to Survival
Save Jerusalem
The Return
Jerusalem D.C.
Purity and Peace of Mind
Who Cries for the Hurting?
Living Fear Free
I Shall Not Want
Let My People Go
Jerusalem Betrayed
Seven Years of Shaking: A Vision
The Nuclear Bomb of Islam
Jerusalem Prophecies
Pray For Peace of Jerusalem
America's War: The Beginning of the End
The Jerusalem Scroll
The Prayer of David
The Unanswered Prayers of Jesus
God Wrestling
The American Prophecies
Beyond Iraq: The Next Move
The Final Move beyond Iraq
Showdown with Nuclear Iran
Jimmy Carter: The Liberal Left and World Chaos
Atomic Iran
Cursed
Betrayed
The Light
Corrie's Reflections & Meditations
The Revolution
The Final Generation
Seven Days
The Locket

GAMECHANGER SERIES:
GameChanger
Samson Option
The Four Horsemen

THE PROTOCOLS SERIES:
The Protocols
The Candidate

Persia: The Final Jihad
Jerusalem
The History of Christian Zionism
Countdown
Ten Boom: Betsie, Promise of God
Commanded Blessing
Born Again: 1948
Born Again: 1967
Presidents in Prophecy
Stand with Israel
Prayer, Power and Purpose
Turning Your Pain Into Gain
Christopher Columbus, Secret Jew
Living in the F.O.G.
Finding Favor with God
Finding Favor with Man
Unleashing God's Favor
The Jewish State: The Volunteers
See You in New York
Friends of Zion: Patterson & Wingate
The Columbus Code
The Temple
Satan, You Can't Have My Country!

COMING SOON:
Satan, You Can't Have Israel!
Netanyahu
Lights in the Darkness

TO PURCHASE, CONTACT: orders@timeworthybooks.com
P. O. BOX 30000, PHOENIX, AZ 85046